My Journey.
My Peace.

Qiana Buckner

PRAISE FOR QIANA BUCKNER'S *MY JOURNEY. MY PEACE.*

My Journey. My Peace. highlights the importance of trusting the process and embracing your unique journey. I appreciate Qiana's transparency about how pain, shame and disappointment can overshadow our successes, accomplishments and accolades if we do not remain focused on our reason WHY.

My Journey. My Peace. is a must read for the young professionals who have experienced any form of adversity while in pursuit of greatness.

~Sharise Nance, LCSW, CCTP,
Best Selling and Award Winning Author

We live in a society that conditions its members to live someone else's reality. So many people leave this physical world without fulfilling God's purpose. . . *My Journey. My Peace.* is an emotional book that takes you through Qiana's journey to find her individual peace and purpose.

As you turn the pages, you will find that every experience made Qiana stronger, but those setbacks made her a better person. I hope that when you read her story that you will find the courage to embrace your journey and abandon other people's reality in order to fulfill God's purpose for your life.

~Sean L. McCaskill, MA Sociology Specialization
Author, Motivational Speaker, Consultant

In *My Journey. My Peace.* Qiana Buckner invites the reader to explore the fragility and strength of the human spirit. Her story is compelling, brave, and authentic.

~Dr. Tricia Shelton, Ed.D.
Author and Educator

My Journey. My Peace.

Qiana Buckner

ISBN-13: 978-1979790109

ISBN-10: 1979790108

A Diamond in the Rough Productions, LLC.

The material contained in this memoir is from the memory of the author. Names have either been used by permission or changed to protect privacy.

1. Memoir. 2. Motivational and Inspirational. 3. Women. 4.Christian Faith.

Editing by InSCRIBEd Inspiration
Book Cover Design by: Denishia Macon, Macon Designs
[www.macondesigns.com]
First Printing October 2017

DEDICATION

- To the man who loved me the best way he knew how, my Dad. I was graciously given your smile and kind heart. You taught me that I should never walk on the outside by a curb and this is a lesson that I'll never forget. I now fully understand the talk we had that day. I hold you in my heart and think of you daily. I know you are smiling down from Heaven. You traded pain and sorrow for joy. I can agree with The Winans' family song, millions didn't make it, but I'm glad that you did. Continue to Rest in Heaven my hero. I will forever love you.

- To my love, my big brother Wesley Dean Quarles Jr., you are one of the biggest parts of me. There are no words that will ever be able to describe the love I hold in my heart for you. No one can, nor will anyone ever take your place. In death, you gave us life. Now I can say, "Amen."

- My AMAZING sons Kevin and Korey you are my lifelines and my heartbeats. When I wanted to give up, the thought of you kept me going. You two are the greatest gifts that God could ever give to me. Thank you for loving mommy unconditionally. I love you both more than life itself. All that I am and everything that I do, I do it for you.

- Grandmother Anna Ruth you were a strong woman full of discipline, confidence, integrity, character and love. You did not say much but you didn't have to – in your silence was brute strength. Your actions proved you to be the woman that I knew and loved so much. You are the wind beneath my wings.

CONTENTS

ACKNOWLEDGMENTS

- I thank my heavenly Father for inspiring me to write this book. God is the lifter of my head and I am grateful for His love, power, anointing, peace, grace and mercy on my life. Without God I could not exist. I give Him all the glory for the great things He has done for me; the voices of a million angels will not be able to express my gratitude. In God I live, in God I trust and in God I have my being.
- To my editor, writing mentor, Scribe Coach and much more, Mrs. Penda L. James. You are the epitome of amazing! I am grateful that God has allowed us to connect. If it had not been for your push and encouragement to finish this book there would be no manifestation of *My Journey. My Peace.* Thank you for our talks on the phone, the emails, prayers and the early morning FB chats. No words will ever be able to express the love and appreciation that I have for you and your company, InSCRIBEd Inspiration. From the bottom of my heart I thank you for believing in me and in my journey.
- Emmy award winning actress and comedienne Mo'Nique, I humbly bow and say, Thank you for teaching me to embrace me – with all of my flaws. You unknowingly have lived your life in such a way that I can believe in, and EMBRACE myself as a woman. You have given me a reason to smile about who I am. I owe that entire part of my journey to you. You always stay true to yourself and you encourage women across the globe by letting us know to love ourselves for free. You are truly indescribable. I look up to you and I salute you my sister, my friend, my inspiration.
- Lastly I want to honor my mom, Frances M. Thank you Mommy for being the woman that you are. This book opens up the world to a piece of our lives. There is nothing about my journey that I would change – it made me who I am today. This is our story for God's Glory so that others may heal. You are truly a Diva and I will never stop loving you.

INTRODUCTION TO THE PROCESS

As I was writing this book, the song "Yet Still I Rise" by Yolanda Adams was on my mind. As I began to tell my side to a story with many characters, I wondered how people would receive my testimony. Although some may argue or disagree with what I write; this is *my* version of *my* story and I poured my heart out while writing.

All of my life, people have assumed they knew how I felt about certain situations. It is even laughable that some people try to tell me how, what or why I should feel, a certain way. They expect me to feel how they would in any given situation. People think they know me, but no one knows my process. I am telling my story from the inside looking out.

What is a process? When we think or talk about a process, it is often related to as a series of different things that happen or take place to get us to the goal or outcome that we are trying to reach. Remember, it's not about the destination; it's about the journey. The destination is the result of not giving up or turning around on the journey. The process is the actual journey that gets you to your specific destination. One dictionary defines the word "process" in this way:

- A series of actions directed towards a specific aim.
- A series of actions that produce change or development.

One thing that I have learned is that everything has, or goes through a process. There is a process for digesting food. There is process for birthing babies and there was a process for me to writing this book. What I've learned about processes is that during them, there is a consistent forward movement. For example, when I am doing weddings or funerals as an event planner, I line the key people up in order for the processional. Do you see the word process in there? Everything has a process.

The process is not the best part of your journey; it actually is what seems to be the longest. Everyone wants to get glory from the story but they tend to forget about the process it takes to achieve victory. On the road to success and victory one must plan for situations that may deter focus. However, be encouraged by Romans 8:28 which says:

> *"And we know that ALL THINGS work together for the good of them who love the Lord and are called according to His purpose."*

On a drive to Florida for a Disney World vacation with my family I learned and experienced how the value of a process brings great rewards. My family drove from Pittsburgh to Orlando during a sixteen-hour expedition. As we made the drive through several states, we had beautiful weather, heavy rain and hail. There were times when fog blinded our vision and we had to determine if we were going to have to pull over. The process that it took to get us to Florida was not easy but it was worth it.

We grew tired and wanted to stop driving, but we kept moving ahead because we kept our destination in our mind. We stopped a couple times to eat. Upon arrival at our destination we were relieved. The trip was really fun for us too. Getting there was not easy but the reward was great.

I would encourage you to never take your process for granted. The process is never an easy place to be, however it is what you make it.

My best friend is working on a Master's degree. I encourage her to think about the end result, not look at where she is. I tell her, "You are going to look back on these current days and smile. It's not easy, but it is definitely worth it." I say the same to you dear reader - you are worth it. How we handle our journey is a choice. God gives us free will. I encourage you to embrace the process. Processes are not meant to break you; they are designed to teach you lessons. During a process you learn gratitude, humility and how to testify. One day you will be able to help someone else get through a process.

After one of my son's football games we had to walk up numerous steps and hills to get back to our car. I encouraged myself because I was tired; *Don't worry about the steps or the hill Qiana. Focus on getting to your vehicle."* Each step was a victory. Not only did it take my mind off of the difficult walk, when I finished, I looked back and saw that it really wasn't so bad. I was grateful that even though I did not like the steps and hills, I was able to walk. Even though I had to pause and breathe along the way, I made it to the car.

I pray that as you go through my journey in this book that you will be inspired and encouraged. I pray that you will read my story and see beauty for ashes, healing, and hidden treasure in your own life experiences. The processes we experience are not always easy but there is always a great reward. There is beauty in the diamond that will come forth as a result of brokenness.

Be inspired today. Be encouraged always.

Love,

~Q~

FOREWORD: A DIAMOND IN THE ROUGH

I am beyond honored to write this Foreword for my spiritual daughter. I chose the topic "A Diamond in the Rough" because this is the name of her ministry.

The creation of a diamond is an act of God. All diamonds start from a lump of black coal. According to the definition found in "Webster's Dictionary," coal is a "black or brownish-black solid combustible substance formed by the partial decomposition of vegetable matter without free access of air and under the influence of moisture and often increased pressure and temperature that is widely used as a natural fuel."

We often admire diamonds because of the shine, luster, and beauty. We wear them in our earrings, engagement rings, and necklaces without realizing the major price or processes that had to be paid. There are many people who have been killed for the sake of getting the prized diamond. In Africa for example, the soil is rich because there are diamonds hidden within her. Some diamonds from Africa are considered "Blood Diamonds" because someone paid for them with their lives.

How could something as beautiful as a diamond come from something decayed? How could God take us, with our messed up selves, and create something beautiful? It is easy for Him because He is God and there is nothing impossible for Him! God will take our mess, our hurt, disappointments, or failures, and put us under pressure to bring forth character, purpose, and destiny.

Don't despise your process. You are not too damaged for God to use you. No dear heart; you are a diamond in the rough. If you surrender your will to the Father you will see transformations in your life that will take you from glory to glory. Never underestimate being like a diamond in the rough because it looks bad right now - in the end, your value will be priceless.

God allows you to go through fiery trials to present you with more anointing, power, and glory! Your enemies can't stop you, or take your shine. God called you forth and chose you for His purpose to shine in the midst of your enemies. Prove to them that God is on your side. Living the "diamond life" means you are able to embrace your process and allow God to get the glory out of every situation. When you give God the glory in all things, it shows that you trust Him to bring you out on top.

I understand what it means to live the "diamond life." As the CEO of my organization, Theta Phi Sigma Christian Sorority, Incorporated, I was designated the name of "White Diamond." God took me through a process for the sake of ministry to put my name to the test! I have endured pseudo friendships, a divorce, and five years of single motherhood. But God! He brought me through it and now I am doing greater things in ministry. God has expanded by boarders and I am remarried to the love of my life. God took me through many hurtful things to teach me how to trust and depend on Him. I paid a price for the wisdom I have beyond my years! Salvation is free but the anointing will definitely cost.

As you read this awesomely anointed book remember to have patience with yourself; God is not through with you. God may have you hidden in the soil for a season like the diamonds in Africa. When your process is complete, He will take you from the soil and polish you. The world will see your beauty.

Jesus paid the ultimate sacrifice for us with His blood. I guess that makes you a "blood diamond" as well. If it were not for the blood of Jesus we would not be who we are today. He suffered for us and now He is seated at the right hand of the Father. We must also endure for His namesake. If we suffer with Him, we will reign with Him.

Don't dim your shine for anyone. You can no longer sing, "this little light of mine" because the anointing on your life is going to cause you to SHINE BIG!

~Apostle, Dr. Jessica Cole

IT WAS PAIN THAT GOT ME HERE

On August 25, 2017 I had a major emotional break down. It was the day of my new website launch and I woke up with great expectations. I want you to know what I was thinking and feeling in the moment so I will share my heart as I wrote it that day.

Pain got me here.

What should be one of the most liberating days of my life has turned out to be tough. Instead of leaping for joy and celebrating an accomplishment, I am in tears and having a break down. My heart is heavy. I am experiencing something different I don't understand.

Today is the official launch of my new and improved website. This is the day that the world: my friends, family, and others will see what *A Diamond in the Rough Productions* is all about.

Yesterday I received crazy emails from my boss letting me know my caseload would expand. I thought to myself, *I'm trying to focus on this launch and she is sending me crazy emails.* I knew today would be hectic at work but why the sadness during such a liberating time?

I have been praying and interceding daily for a friend. I knew that this friend was my assignment. I have prayed and cried out to God repeatedly. But today is just different. To me, this friend is different today too. My website has launched and my friend is supposed to announce his upcoming website launch too. Why am I not excited? I have been trying to reach my friend and can't find him. I have sent him text messages, and he hasn't responded. I am hurt by his non-responsiveness so I am sitting in my truck in the front of my house. Several thoughts are running through my mind.

God, I'm supposed to be happy. Am I feeling what he is going through? You know when I intercede for people that I begin to feel what they feel. When they hurt I hurt. If they are depressed I get sad. I pray that the feeling lifts off of me, so God lift it off of him.

I am praying like I've never prayed for anyone in my life; my heart is tender and I am crying out to God. As I sit in my truck before going inside my house I can't stop the racing thoughts. *God what is he going through? I know, I did it again. I put someone else before myself. I put my feelings and my heart out there prematurely. You know I'm a giver, but when I am ignored or left hanging I feel abandoned. You told me to pray for him. You told me that this was my assignment. Why is this happening?*

My sons are with their father. I have plans to finish the last two chapters of my book in the dining room. Why am I on social media! My friend is online as he often is but he still hasn't answered me! I feel hurt and rejected. God what is this really? The tears fall again, and this time, they come hard. *God forgive me for anything that I have done that has caused me to feel any emotions toward my friend that I should not feel. I thought that I heard You speak to me about this person, but did I hear wrong? I am tired of always being the one to pray and give. I need a covering too. I need someone to pour back into me! I did it again God, and I'm so sorry.*"

I am so emotional right now! I can't help but think about my lifelines – my two sons. Today is Friday and school is starting on Monday. I haven't been school shopping and my boys need school clothes and supplies. I am always done early when it comes to things like this. My oldest son just asked me this morning, "When are we getting new school clothes?"

My tears forcefully fall. *But God, I just left corporate America and took a huge pay cut. I prayed and I was obedient when you spoke to me. But now, I find myself in a bind. I now realize that no amount of money is worth your sanity or peace of mind. How do I find myself in this place of hurt? I need clarity about a few things. Did I hear you right?*

As is my normal reaction I am now in survivor mode. I am thinking of what I am going to do and what I need to do to make it through the first week of school. I really just cannot believe it. Here I am crying, breaking down, and I can't shake this feeling of hurt inside. I am supposed to be celebrating today!

Why is my sister calling at 4:34 p.m.? Ebony Moultrie, this is my close sister in Christ. She is so cheerful on the phone, "Hey how are you?"

"I'm ok. How are you?" I am trying so hard to avoid the conversation. I really don't feel like talking right now.

"What's wrong? Something is not right. I felt your spirit. YOU KNOW God would not have laid it on my heart to call you during this part of the day unless something is up with you."

I can't fake it any longer. I have to empty my entire heart to Ebony. I need to tell her about everything that is going on in my life including my marriage and what I need for

> my children. Of course Ebony is a good sister, she knows how to pick me up and encourage me with the Word of the Lord. As she is talking God is showing me why it is necessary for this breakdown to happen in this moment. It is necessary for me to shed all of these tears and cry out to God today because He wants me to be transparent for others to see Him.

My breakdown on August 25, 2017 gave me the revelation that I would have to start from the end of my story so that you as my reader can understand the beginning of my peace. We have to start from the most recent part of my process before we go back to the beginning. I have been running from peace a long time. In order to be transparent I have to be willing to open up, and expose myself so that you may be healed, delivered, and set free.

I invite you to open your heart to me as I share with you the long journey toward my peace.

PART I: MATURE DIAMOND

GOD SPOKE THROUGH A DREAM

June 7, 2016

I was treated horribly for no reason at all while working in corporate America. It got so bad that I was starting to experience daily physical ailments. On this particular day, I went upstairs to my bedroom, dropped my laptop bag, my purse, and fell face down on my bed. I was tired physically, spiritually, mentally, and emotionally and I had a headache. I ended up falling asleep across the bed and having an interesting dream.

In my dream I saw a house that I knew represented the church my husband I and were attending. Inside of the house there was no peace due to everyone (including the Pastor) fighting or arguing. I turned to walk outside of the house but as I was walking to the door, I recognized a female member of the church arguing with someone I could not see as she was walking outside.

Upon further observation I saw that she was actually arguing with me. It was odd that I was wearing shorts and a t-shirt and she was literally dressed as if she was getting ready to walk down the aisle to get married. Standing beside the woman I saw her groom who was donned in a black and white tuxedo. The woman, who I knew in real life, had recently gotten married. In my dream her groom was someone she had been sleeping with prior to being married; he was not her husband.

When I realized who she was and that she was arguing with me, I called her by name and tried to diffuse the situation. "Go ahead" I told her, "I don't want to argue with you." I despise conflict in my life and I don't do drama. I have no time for arguing or fighting therefore I usually bow out gracefully from conflict.

The woman kept arguing, instigating, and nagging me. When I got fed up with her I did what I was always afraid of doing; I grabbed her and we started fighting. I beat the women up in her wedding gown to the point of banging her head off of the steps. Her husband stood by and did nothing. He acted as if he was not even there while his wife was fighting.

After the fight was over, the woman was crying and bleeding yet her dress remained clean. A crowd of people came to console her. A few people in the crowd looked at me as if I had done something wrong. I just kept saying out loud, "I didn't do anything." I was trying to explain myself, "She started it."

The crowd led her across the street. Someone called the police and I became a wanted criminal for defending myself. I was afraid and nervous about police looking for me. I saw my youngest niece who said, "I wonder what your kids will think."

"Leave my kids out of it!" I snapped at her. I ran into the house and saw my oldest son sitting in the living room. We made eye contact before I ran up the stairs. I found a hammer and nails and started to board up the windows and doors to hide from the police. When I got tired and stopped hammering I realized that I was tired of more than just hammering. I was tired of running; tired of hiding.

I had nothing to hide from, this woman started conflict with me and I stood up against her attacks. I decided to turn myself in to the police. I walked back outside and saw the woman across the street still being dramatic. I walked toward the corner and saw parked police cars. A woman got out of her car and stopped me. “Wait, don't turn yourself in. You didn't do anything wrong.” She handed me two books and said, "Here, read these.”

That is when I woke up from my dream.

As most prophets do, I began to pray for interpretation from the Holy Spirit in order to analyze my dream. I focused on understanding what God wanted to show me about the girl in the wedding dress. My eyes were closed as I was praying and as my mind was trying to analyze my dream, I saw a vision of myself standing on top of a tall skyscraper. I was going to jump. I began to question, "Am I going to die? Is this going to be my demise? Is this the way I'm supposed to go? Before I could finish the questions, I jumped from the building.

There are myths that when people fall from high places in dreams that they die. One myth is that you die while you’re in the air before you hit the ground. As I was falling and getting closer, at the ground something happened. I saw the Holy Spirit. He allowed my flesh to hit the ground, but He was at the bottom waiting for me with His arms outstretched; he caught my spirit. As my flesh hit the ground I lay on my side, but my spirit was caught and carried by God.

I opened my eyes. I said to God, “I'm not sure what any of that meant or what you’re doing, but Lord, please just give me the interpretation of this dream.

THE TRANSITION

June 8, 2016

Something dramatic happened that changed the course of my life on this day. I was back at work and it was a usual day in the office. I had sent a message to a friend about something for my sons. This friend and I hardly ever talked but we had been friends for about 21 years. Whenever we talked, we would catch each other up on our lives. The conversation that day was not like the others. It was so fun and it lasted much longer than all of the other conversations - 10 hours longer with a few breaks in between. At the time, I thought nothing of it. We laughed and talked about our children, our Godchildren, family and friends. At that point in my life, I was strong in my faith, loved my family and I could say life was good. This friend whom I had known for years wanted to continue the conversation on a deeper level and I agreed.

The next day I saw the person face-to-face. We continued our conversation but it was different. The tables had turned. This person began to tell me how he had felt about me all of these years. He said, "You can't even look at me."

Being the strong woman I said, "Boy please." I looked him, in his eyes and that is when he began to say more than the right words. He began to speak to the woman in me and beyond. He encouraged, inspired, and loved on me with powerful words at the same time. I felt something from the inside out. I was in his presence, and he was saying all of these amazing things and making me feel loved and wanted. My mind and my thoughts immediately shifted to my husband. I heard this man's voice, but my heart began to question, *Why doesn't my husband make me feel like this? I want this to come from my husband, not this guy. I mean he and I are cool, but I love my husband. He is my world.*

I was confused and it was a weird place. I had this wonderful feeling that I had never felt before yet it didn't come from the one that I loved and gave my "I do." My life as I knew it had taken a detour. Although I entertained the conversation with my friend, I did not respond right away because I knew in my heart I wanted so badly for it to be my husband romancing me and not some friend who I barely made contact with on a regular basis.

I went home after work, after the conversation and I told my husband everything. I told him what happened to me. I told him about the conversation and how it made me feel. I told him how passionate it was and how romantic it was and how all I wanted was for it to be coming from him. I questioned, "Why did I feel like that from him?"

The response that I got was, "Yeah, I agree, we are lacking intimacy". I felt as if my feelings were pushed to the side. I was crying out as I had done so many times not even realizing it was going to be met with the same type of response, a nonchalant attitude and as if I my feelings didn't matter. I felt unprotected from the one I was committed to be with forever.

After our brief conversation about my day and what happened, I went on about my usual activities. But I had been changed. Could it have been the feeling of being rejected? I didn't know. I began to question within myself, *Does my husband hear me? Does he even care? So many things good bad or indifferent have happened in our marriage that no one knows about or knows how we feel about it.*

People can, and will make assumptions, but there will always be multiple sides to a story. My husband and I continued on in our daily lives. I offered counseling as I had done countless times in the past. My husband would always refuse to go, "I don't need counseling." What is it with men and counseling? That's another story for another day.

Things in my personal life seemed to just get worse and worse. Just when I thought it couldn't get any worse, what was already a crazy hell bound experience at work took a turn for the worst. Everything around me seemed to be going haywire. My migraine headaches got even more intense. I was crying almost daily, not knowing how to feel bout anything anymore because of one conversation. I started expressing to my husband again how unhappy I was at work. I wanted and needed a change in all areas of my life. I was met with the usual, "What do you want? I'm Busy. I'm working." Or "Leave me alone, I don't feel like talking." I would cry and pray, and then pray and cry. I reached out to people in leadership who I loved and trusted.

It's funny how God began to open my eyes while I was in transition. I began to discern and see where God's "elite" is truly coming from. After pouring out my heart with the truth, one woman of God asked me, "Well is your husband beating you?"

"Of course not" I was incensed, "He would never do that."

She responded, "Well, then there is no reason to question or even think about leaving."

It really was that serious for me. I was contemplating so many things at the time. Another friend in ministry began to ask questions and wanted to know every single detail. I obliged and she had no advice or encouragement. She simply just wanted to know. And the weirdest one of all is when I was told by someone, "Show and teach your husband how to be a covering. You are in leadership and have gone through training." She told me that I was responsible to teach him! It is not my job to teach him how to be the head of the household or my covering.

At this point, life for me was getting a little worse and even ridiculous. But in the midst of all of this craziness, here was this person, still saying all of the right things. My best friend and her husband told me to stop talking to him. She advised that I could no longer be his friend. They would pray for my husband and me.

At the time I felt like I was drifting further and further away from life and all it had to offer. I was walking around just existing. I was confused by this romance from my friend since I had never been romanced before.

I started writing in my journal all of the things that I had been going through and all of the things that I wanted to express to my husband. These were my honest feelings about everything that I felt were unanswered or not dealt with in our marriage. I finally got the courage and strength to go to him again about this person and all that was going on with us. I asked if we could talk. It was met with the same detached responses. I stood my ground, "This is very important that you and I talk about this." With frustration, he agreed. I began to read everything to him that I had written in my journal. I reminded him about how I had felt over the years. I shared how I felt unprotected and how my trust in him was lacking. I talked about how I had been feeling over the last few weeks and how I could not fathom why an intimate conversation could make me feel wanted, loved, intimate and protected.

Spiritual Warfare

For several weeks, my spiritual warfare increased on all levels. I was in a place that I had never been before. Prior to that time I was always the good girl of my crew. I was the strong one that everybody leaned on when they were looking for answers and help. I was the listening ear or the shoulder that everyone around me could cry on. What I thought would be a simple conversation with a friend had me out of whack.

After reading my thoughts and pouring out my heart to my husband, his response remained unchanged. He was saying one thing and I was saying another. I said to him, "This is why we need a counselor or a mediator, because you can't see where I'm coming from and I don't understand where you are coming from." I expressed again, "I don't understand how someone else can make me feel a certain way and I want it to be you."

When I spoke those words he gave me a different response. "If he makes you feel like that, then you need to go and be with him then." I was in total shock. The feeling that I felt at that moment is indescribable. I felt as if my soul had left my body. The rejection that I felt at that point was too much to handle and I was tired. I was shocked but most of all injured. I asked him, "Did you just tell me to go and be with another man?"

"Yes, I did." That moment was my breaking point in my marriage and in my life at thirty-eight years old. I couldn't believe what I had heard. At that moment, the conversation ended. I got up and went upstairs to my bedroom. I shut the door and cried some of the hardest tears I had ever cried. Although this wasn't the first time we had an exchange like this, it was the first time something on the inside of me was shifted. I was already going through so much in every area of my life: work, church, home and as I was crying I told God, "I am tired! I tried and I'm tired of trying. "

I knew that I wanted to be happy. I wanted and needed to live, but not like this. I told myself, for the first time in my life, *I am going to do whatever it takes to make me happy. No longer am I going to live for anyone else. No longer am I going to live through anyone else. I am going to see the world through Qiana's eyes from now on, and I promise myself that I will live.*

The growth that occurred in me that day gave me boldness I had never had before. I was becoming my own person, and it was scary. I didn't know exactly what that meant or how I was going to do it, but I knew in order for me to survive another moment, I had to choose myself over anyone else this time. That is the moment the journey began. Because of this particular situation, I began to realize as a woman what I really wanted and who I really am. It was then that I began to realize that my life is important. It was then that I began to realize if I don't take care of myself, I can't take care of anyone else. God was using that moment to give me beauty for ashes. I love the song that Tye Tribbet sings about it.

After that conversation, my statements and posture all became unified, "I want to live, and I'm going to live." My husband was distant toward me and I was weary of it. For many years we argued about and discussed the same things. For years I accepted the fact that he was just not going to defend or protect me. In life and even marriage, you have to pick and choose your battles, and after years of fighting, I told him and others, "There were two battles that I surrendered to because they were non-negotiable when it came to our relationship. That was the battle of the church and family. Why get in the ring to fight knowing that you are just going to go around in circles and eventually give up or be defeated anyway?

My mind was reprogrammed for one thing and one thing only, living for and loving Qiana. My journey to love me and live for me has not been easy. It started out quite bumpy. You see, I thought in the beginning because I was hurting, I was just going to do what I wanted and anything that I could to make me physically happy. In order for a person to live and be happy, they have to first know what it is that makes them happy. I had to find that for myself. I had to literally get to know me and I made some mistakes along the way. Surely this wasn't the "me" that I wanted, and so desperately needed to find. But when you are on a journey to finding yourself, you don't just find the good, you meet ALL of you: the good, the bad, and the ugly.

A SETBACK IN MY FAITH

While growing in the confidence of myself I made a physical mistake. I hate to admit that I ended up having a short affair. With a bad decision I fell into temptation. I thought that because my friend was entertaining my mind with wonderful sentiments that caused me to feel loved, appreciated as a mom, as a person, and as a woman. I followed what felt was right for me at the time. Long or short, an affair is wrong on every level. I can tell you the truth, having an affair doesn't solve anything. It actually made me feel worse about myself. Yes, I wanted to live and be happy but not at the expense of hurting others. My husband did not deserve that from me. In my heart I don't like to hurt people. I cringe at the thought. Through it all, my husband is an amazing person. He is a phenomenal father to our children and yet we both struggled in the capacity of our marriage.

After church one Sunday my husband and I went downstairs to say hello to everyone, which was our ritual. I was having a conversation with a young woman who was openly homosexual. This young lady had a tongue ring that you could see when she spoke. After our conversation ended, I started another conversation with the Pastor. We said our usual hello, but the conversation got interesting.

He had seen me talking to the young lady and he began to talk about tongue rings and how he knew why women wore them. That is not a conversation that he should have been having with me. Normally, I have listened and laughed it off, but I responded to him, "I am just trying to live." That was my answer for everything. I was in survivor mode. I personally did not care about tongues or rings and why the girl who had just left had one. His response to me was "You should live. You are always taking care of everyone else. You need to start living and doing for Qiana."

That sounds great right? Well the next statement took me for a loop. He said, "You can go and be out there and live it up, but don't go too far. I mean you can even get on the stripper pole." Here is where you insert the shocked emoji eyes. I couldn't believe he said that to me. My husband was standing there with me and he chuckled a bit. But the Pastor must have seen my facial expression because he then said, "Well, the only person you need to be on a pole for is Coach." In my mind I was thinking again, *technical foul.* I didn't see the humor or even the sense in what he was saying. I knew at that moment that I was never going to step my foot back in that place again. God was showing me through that conversation with the pastor that I was changing - growing in my journey to find me. I was becoming a little exhausted and frustrated with the process, the journey I was on to find me, but I knew it had to be done.

A few days later I was praying in the shower when I began to talk openly to God. I began to repent and tell Him how sorry I was for my actions. "What am I supposed to do God? What am I supposed to do in my marriage? I want things to be better but I also want to grow. It seems the more I grow, the more I decide to love me and live for me, the worse things get. The more I discover that we are just two different people, on two very different planes, going in two different directions I don't know what I am supposed to do."

God answered me and said, "Prepare to land on your feet." I

didn't understand what that meant but I knew I was going to land on my feet and I had to prepare for it.

I took from that prayer time instructions to pour myself back into God. I began to study and pray more. Believe it or not, there were many other things that could take a whole new book to describe. Pouring myself back into God and Him pouring back into me, I finally was on the right path to finding and living for myself.

HEALING BEGINS

As time passed after the church conversation and my prayer in the shower, God began to show me different things about myself, my marriage, and how healing needed to take place for the both of us prior to us coming together in holy matrimony. That year when everything happened, I was turning thirty-nine. I finally realized that for thirty years, I've actually been on this journey. I had also been through major trauma. I was seeing a therapist. She was also an associate pastor, but she was licensed and had a degree in counseling and therapy. We didn't know each other.

In our first session, she asked me a series of personal questions about my life, my background, and what brought me to her. I answered truthfully; I will never be ashamed of my past. I am proud of who I am and where I came from. But during this first session, after listening to me, she looked at me and said two things that still stick out to me to this day: "If anyone ever asks you if you have ever experienced trauma, don't you ever tell them 'No, you say yes."

I looked at her incredulously and asked her, "Did I say no to that question"?

"Yes. You did."

I was so used to being strong. Every time I told my story, the hurt and trauma was brushed under the rug. My attitude was always, "Yes, it happened but I'm good, I'm over it. I made it through." In finding me, I had to admit, "Yes, I am broken, and yes I am healed. " It wasn't the fact that I had never admitted the things that happened in my life; it was just that I was strong and I dealt with them the best way that I knew how. It was such an eye opener for me at that moment. Then she said, "You have never in your life had a covering. Not from your father, not from any pastor, and not even from your husband."

That was another eye opener. I left that appointment with a new outlook on my circumstances and my situation. It was as if God had taken blinders off of my eyes and I was able to see. I was finally making progress with loving and living for me. In order to know the history of a tree, you must know the seed that was planted and follow the root.

I was on my journey to peace but I still had to face reality that my job at the time was draining the life that I had left in me. I had migraines all day everyday. I was targeted and picked on for no reason. I had wanted to leave for years but my husband convinced me to stay. I had to stay, even though everything was pointing to and confirming that I needed and should have been gone a long time ago. The money was good and we had just bought a house. I knew that if I had stayed, I was going to be fired or laid off; it was an uneasy season of corporate America.

I remember after one crazy day at work that I pulled into my garage and God spoke to me, "You're in transition." Again, I didn't understand it at the time. I just said as I always did, "Ok God." I knew that transition meant movement of some sort and I left it at that. Yet again, after God spoke, things began to shift in my life again. My husband wanted me to stay because of the longevity and the finances. I took my first leap of faith while on the journey and decided to leave my job. I decided that my peace of mind, my health, and my sanity were far greater than any amount of money. Of course, I asked myself, *Are you sure?* I kept asking God, "Did I hear you right?" He just kept saying the same thing over and over telling me that I was in transition.

I left that job and with the help of one of my dearest friends I found another place to work. Although I took a pay cut I had a consistent schedule, and my journey - my peace could be solidified. I am comfortable in saying that was the best decision for me.

While all of these things were happening in my marriage, I maintained my role as a year round sports mom. I kept my responsibilities as the Vice President of a wonderful Charter School, ran and operated my events management company, and I crossed over into membership of one of the greatest Christian sororities on this side of heaven. All of this and I was still going through this fire that was seemingly getting hotter. Yet I was still holding my head above ground.

I have always known that I was going to write a book. I just didn't know what I was going to write about. I had no clue what I was going to say or who my audience would be. What was this book going to be about? So many times throughout the years, I would see things or hear something and thought that I had a title to my book. But God would always say, "That's not it."

That dream on June 7, 2016 was showing me that my life would change forever. It was months later in the midst of turmoil that I would arrive home and walk through my door, that God would whisper the words: "My Journey, My Peace." As soon as He said it, I knew that was the title to my first book and chapters began to flow. There were late nights and early mornings. There have been tears, prayers, and pain, but this is my journey.

A journey is a faith walk. Every move that I have made, I've had to trust solely on God and God alone. Everyone has a journey.

We are all on different roads, going in different directions trying to reach our destiny. Many of us will end up reaching it, and others may stop and break down along the way. No matter what anyone else says or thinks, you must keep going. This journey is a personal one between you and God. I employ you to travel the journey and LIVE through the process. Will there be detours, traffic, and construction along the way? Absolutely but you must keep moving forward.

As a teenager at St. Paul AME Zion Church I heard the phrase, "Bend, Don't Break." Pastor Jackie Dewberry preached a sermon with that title and it struck a chord in my heart that day. I did not know, how that particular phrase would become a forever part of my life.

As most people would already expect, life has its ups and downs. It has trials and triumphs, victories and defeats. Society would define a normal life for a child as one who lives in a two-parent household, 2.5 children, a pet and finances to boot. I could beg to differ. If that was and is the norm, my life has never been normal or as average as one would think.

I read a book by Monica Hawkins, an associate and entrepreneur, entitled "A Shattered Heart, A Journey of Hope, Trust and Healing." In her book she talked about the healing process after the tragedy of the death of her son. She talked about mourning a tragic loss from a mother's perspective. Although I have never experienced the death of a child, her testimony helped me too. Monica's book taught me how to be transparent. During that time, we were kindred spirits. I had lost my brother; different kinship, but still a deep hurt and grief.

Writing my story has now become part of my healing. Since I was a child I have always wanted a voice. I always wanted to tell my side of the story and be part of the decision making process. I just never responded much to what people had to say and that led people to believe that they had me figured out. I still don't respond much to what I see, which is definitely beyond what people are saying about me.

Honestly I don't think people would have been able to comprehend my responses. I don't think that people would have believed me if I told them that I could see right through them. Yet I have decided as always to take the high road. Now begins my transparency. Welcome to the other side of the story.

PART II: A DIAMOND IN THE ROUGH

THE "GOOD 'OLE DAYS"

Growing up, we didn't have much money but those were the good ole days. Yeah, back in those days life seemed good because we didn't know any better. There was food, there was fun, there was family, and there was love. What I did not realize was the food that we ate came from food banks or was purchased with the help of public assistance. As an adult I learned that history repeats itself when I realized that my mom had kids on welfare and was living in the projects. I never knew that we struggled. In my childhood innocence I didn't know anything about welfare.

I was born the third of four children. My mom birthed two boys and two girls. I was living with both of my parents in Arlington Heights, an urban project development in the South Hills of Pittsburgh.

My mom had sister girlfriends who loved us as their own children. She loved their children as her own also. To this day, one would never know that we were not blood related because we are still living out our family legacy of connection. We still call one another cousins and no one will ever be able to tell us different. We were raised as a family. We played together, laughed together; we cried together and we fought together (even fought each other). An unbreakable bond was instilled in us.

My parents were both only children, so we did not have aunts or uncles. Unless we told you, you would never know that Aunt Debbie, Aunt Sheila, Aunt Linda, or Aunt Cat (which was short for Catherine) were not blood relatives. There was such a strong bond of love between my mom and her friends. I would remember days when our families would get together for cookouts, while the kids played games like freeze tag, hop scotch, or release the den in the neighborhood court yard. I was one of the younger cousins and one of my fondest memories as a child is when my cousin Michelle taught me how to jump rope between two ropes. She coached me and cheered me on when I finally was able to jump Double Dutch.

Life eventually made an immediate change. It feels like yesterday that my mom and dad were arguing consistently. I remember my dad was no longer in the house a lot because of that. I remember standing outside of our apartment building being introduced to a lady who started coming around us more often. The more she was there the less we saw of my dad and my Grandma.

My maternal grandmother lived in the Hill District of Pittsburgh. She had been there when the Hill District was in the prime of its existence and when history was being made there. We would go to her house on weekends and just be free. We always had fun at home with our cousins, but at Grandma's house, we let loose. The first thing we did was eat so much food that our stomachs hurt.

With this new presence in our midst, it was not too often that we got to enjoy a visit with our grandmother. Those visits would soon become just a memory. I was six years old, and this lady's presence was more visible than ever. She changed the course of what I knew was normal. A few months after she moved in, we were alienated from pretty much everyone. I remember having to sneak away to say hi to all of our aunts and cousins whom we missed dearly. We were not allowed to even look in their direction.

My dad and grandmother were no longer allowed around us. No one familiar was allowed near us anymore, even my mom's sister friends were chased away. No more late nights of hearing their laughter and love for one another.

Shortly after meeting this woman she moved in with us. We were told to call her, "Aunt Ozzie." This aunt was nowhere near as loving, funny, or affectionate as my other aunts. To my surprise, she was the complete opposite. Instead of love came hurt, instead of laughter came pain. I remember when she moved in, she would always say, "You are bad children." She would make comments like, "You are rotten because you are spoiled."

There was verbal abuse from her but eventually it became more drastic. There is a line to be drawn between chastising a child and abusing a child. My sister was eleven and she would get the most abuse. My oldest brother Wesley was seven, I was six and Nathan, our youngest brother was four at the time the physical abuse started in our lives. We were beaten so badly that the beatings left physical scars and bruises on our bodies.

I remember using the restroom at school one day and seeing black and blue marks on my body. Bruises soon became normal - seeing them was a reminder of what had happened that morning, or the day before. Scars resulted from sticks, belt buckles, extension cords, or anything else she could find. I cringe as I remember those thick black and blue marks today. No matter how you look at it, abuse is abuse and no matter what age, no one should ever have to live through it.

United in Marriage

One night, I was outside in front of our building playing. A Caucasian man with glasses and curly sandy brown hair dressed in jeans and a polo shirt came to our building. I noticed him because let's face it; you did not typically see Caucasian men in the projects at night. He stopped and greeted me. I said "Hello," but kept playing. This man was going to our apartment to see my mom and "Aunt Ozzie" to discuss their marriage to one another. I learned that the man was a homosexual minister. We did not know that my mom and Aunt Ozzie had become lovers. My siblings and I were subjected to that lifestyle in 1982, long before it became popular. Our house was the talk of the town and my mom was called names that I had never heard before.

A few days after seeing this man, there were limousines, tuxedos, heart shaped wedding cakes, and a gown. They had a full-blown wedding. I remember the two limos lined up outside. "Aunt Ozzie" wore a gray tuxedo with tails. Her best man, who was also a woman, wore a tuxedo. My mom wore a beautiful gown. There was a beautiful tiered wedding cake. My siblings and I were not able to attend the wedding. That weekend, we had an excuse to finally spend the weekend at my grandmother's house.

In my recollection of that day I was watching the clock. I kept wondering what was going on as the hours passed by. I wondered what my mom was doing, how she was getting ready, or when they arrived at the church. At 3:30 p.m. all I could think was, *It's happening, my mom is getting married.*

113 HABERMAN STREET

About a year after my mother's wedding, we moved out of Arlington Heights. What I would miss the most about leaving that place was our aunties and cousins, the sense of family. We were supposed to be moving to a better place but the fact that it was raining when we moved should have told me otherwise. I remember seeing all of our things in the dumpster including our beds and mattresses. We were told we were going to get brand new stuff.

Our new address was 113 Haberman Street. It was a three-bedroom house with a living room, dining room, kitchen, basement, and attic. I remember "Aunt Ozzie" always telling everyone how much money we had and how we lived in Mt. Washington. The new neighborhood was considered to be "upscale." She made it seem as if we were rich but that was a lie. My mom was the only one in the house who worked. She was an LPN working in various nursing homes. Because of that, we were left with the difficult task of being cared for by the woman who physically abused us.

We slept on the floor on sheets the entire time that we lived in that house. My sister and I shared a room with one dresser in it. My two brothers shared a room with one dresser in it. On cold nights we all slept in the same room by the vents on the floor to keep warm and cuddle under the sheets. We would sometimes have conversations through the vents between the four of us. While we slept on the floor, my mom and "Aunt Ozzie" slept in a king size waterbed in a fully furnished room.

My siblings and I were forced to eat breakfast and lunch at school. For dinner we were only allowed one hot dog and we had to split a can of corn between the four of us. We were not allowed downstairs or in the kitchen. We had to stay in our rooms or in the attic. On the weekends we relied on free lunch programs in the community for breakfast and lunch. During winter months, we were given one bowl of cornflakes to eat. We were given a time limit to eat the cereal or it was thrown away.

I hated when the beatings occurred. My mother's lover kept a thick white stick with blue paint at the tip. The belt buckles and extension cords were no walk in the park either. Once I was tied to the banister on the steps and to the basement poles. That was part of our punishment for being what she called bad kids. My brothers and I used to show each other our scars and compare them.

We were beat for everything. If we touched food in the house, if we came out of our room without them telling us to come out, we were beat. When we were beaten, it felt like torture.

When they would go party at night, they threatened us to stay in our rooms. They would mark the food and other things around the house. We would still sneak out of our rooms and split a few pieces of bread between the four of us because they didn't mark it. We would often find ourselves doing things like that to get food. We were always made to go to the store and go shopping. We would walk from Haberman Street near the South Hills Junction to a Foodland store in Mount Oliver, which was at least four miles. It was a long walk for children. On the way there we would ask people for quarters.

With our money we would buy treats and eat them before we got home. If we did not have enough quarters or even sometimes when we did, we would open up packs of chocolate chips or other things in the store and eat them. We knew if we got caught, it meant big trouble and big pain. Instead of walking around the store with snacks and food, we would open it up and leave the food particle in its place and just continuously come back to the opened package for more. Thank God we never got caught.

I remember walking to the recreational center everyday with my siblings to stand in line to get a free lunch. A lot of times we were bullied because we were there. We were bullied because we were made to wear clothes that were too small but we didn't have a choice about going to get free meals. We were hungry and we were beaten at home if we chose not to go. One day coming back from the free lunch program. We were laughing and playing with one another. I was running and looking back at the same time and then BAM! The left side in the back of my head hit a rusty pole. It hurt so badly.

I grabbed my head and looked at my hand and saw blood. I lost it and started crying. I couldn't believe that I had hit my head and it was bleeding! We went home and I tried to get cleaned up. My older brother asked if I was ok and I didn't answer him so he got mad. I was mad too. I was mad that my siblings had made fun of me for crying at the sight of blood. My way of getting back at him was not to answer his question.

His response made my insides sink. "I'm telling Aunt Ozzie." I surely did not want her to know that I was mad at them and her. Well, told her is what he did. He came back outside and I was summoned upstairs. She hit me so hard that I tumbled back down the steps. Our family dog Omen ran to protect me from a nasty fall from the landing. I still to this day don't know who gave him that name. Omen was a Doberman pinscher and he was true to his nature: protective and loving, a great dog. Whenever we were getting beat, which was quite often, he would try to help and shield us in the process and they would beat him too.

Aunt Ozzie pressed a wet towel extra hard against my head and said, “Shut up. It isn’t that bad.”

MY BOO BEAR

We called Wesley "Boo", or "Boo Bear." He was diagnosed with a disease at birth called Sickle Cell Anemia. They say one in every four African American children are diagnosed with this disease or can be passed the trait if one of their parents has it. It would not be until years later that I would come to grips with and get a real understanding of this deadly and rare disease.

It was a known factor in our house and a normal thing that "Boo" was sick. He would always have painful outbreaks. It was always his legs, or his arms or his back that would hurt. Whenever he was in pain he would be down for a good while at least a week or more. He would miss school but just like at home, the teachers and school administrators knew that he was sick and always understood. Children's Hospital of Pittsburgh was his second home because Wesley would often need blood transfusions.

"Boo" and I were eleven months apart. He was born January 7, 1977. I was born in December of the same year. We were so close in age that we stayed the same age for almost a month. We were in the same grade and went to Carmalt Elementary School. Even though none of us were allowed to have friends, Wesley and I met teachers and fellow students who would become life long friends as well as remain in our hearts and lives forever. We were isolated from everyone and we were not allowed to speak to anyone except each other.

No one at school knew that we had bruises or marks on our bodies. Although Boo was very sick, he was not exempt from torment on his body or beatings. But he was strong, we all were. He was as strong as a kid could be going through so much. Going to Carmalt, we were able to see the outside world. It had been a few years since we had been able to see any family. There was no one to protect us from the bullying we endured inside and outside of the home.

Boo was different. I don't think that kids picked on him as much because everyone knew he was sick. He looked like a normal skinny kid who loved sports, the Pittsburgh Steelers, wrestling and boxing. His favorite boxer was Mike Tyson. He loved the Incredible Hulk so much and he actually got a chance to meet the real Lou Ferrigno - the original Hulk because of special programs for kids who were ill. A lot of times he was the only one allowed to go on the ventures. But one Sunday after church we came home and were surprised to see sitting in our living room a HUGE man with a smile to match waiting to meet my brother and take us all to the amusement park in Pittsburgh, Kennywood Park. That man was Darryl Simms, a Pittsburgh Steeler He was delighted to meet us, especially my brother.

Darryl took us to the park. We all split up into groups: Boo and me stayed with Darryl. Nathan stayed with my mom, and my sister was able to go and be with Ozzie's biological daughter. I chuckle to this day every time I think about Darryl. He was awesome and we loved spending time with him. He got on all the rides with us. I can still hear his laugh and scream as we got soaked on a water ride called the Log Jammer. After the day was over, I remember watching the interview on Channel 11 news and Darryl talked about what a great time he had with us and even said our names on television. He talked about my brother and what a wonderful kid he was.

The week of February 13, 1987 had started normally, however, there are things that I distinctly remember. On Tuesday, February 10th, it was a cold day and Boo could not find his gloves. We were on our way to school and we started running late. Aunt Ozzie began to threaten and tell him how bad she was going to beat him if he didn't find his gloves.

Boo was afraid and he was crying. I helped him find his gloves in his room and we were both happy he was spared from a beating. It was hard seeing him go through his regular pain and of course the beatings did not help. He was so happy and grateful, that he gave me a kiss on my cheek and thanked me.

On February 11th, we were told to stay in our rooms as they went out for the night. We did our usual sneaking and split bread between us. The next day, Aunt Ozzie went into the refrigerator and claimed that her pie had been eaten. I didn't even know that there was a pie in the refrigerator as I had rarely gone in that forbidden place. I knew for a fact that none of my siblings had gone in there or had eaten this pie either. She would eat things and either forget or just blame us for a reason to beat us.

No one could explain who ate this pie. And for some reason, it was serious. We were all called downstairs one by one as if to testify. We each had to explain and tell the truth about where this pie went. After each of us told our story, we were to get beat because a piece of the pie was missing. Each beating was hard. My sister was tied up for hers, and I was held up and stretched out in the air by my siblings for mine. As always, it left marks and bruises.

After the beatings were over, we all had to walk from our house to the store in a snowstorm for a one-inch piecrust. Walking miles to Foodland was sometimes dreadful. In cold weather it was especially hard. This was one particular trip that I will never forget because it changed our hearts and our lives forever. We put on our coats and headed to the Foodland. We got the pie crust only to get home and find out we got the wrong one. My sister, Boo, and me were told to walk back to the store. My younger brother Nathan got to stay home because of the freezing temperatures. He was too young and too small to be walking such a long distance in the cold.

On our walk back from the store the second time that day I looked over at Boo. I watched him walk home in his blue winter coat and scarf. He had on brown corduroy pants and blue sneakers. He seemed fine. When we made it back home it had already started getting dark. Thank God we made it home safe and sound. When we got home, there was a man that we didn't know eating dinner.

It was probably because of their company that we were allowed to eat Sloppy Joes instead of a hotdog. We did have to split a can of corn as our vegetable. As soon as we walked in the door and took our coats off, Boo started shaking. He began to shake so hard that his teeth were chattering. At first, we thought that he was cold from being outside so long. We went into the kitchen to stand at the counter to eat because we weren't allowed to sit at the table. Boo was shaking uncontrollably. My mom gave him instructions, "Stand by the heater. You're probably cold from the walk. Get an aspirin and lie down after you eat."

Ozzie was furious because she had company and was greatly embarrassed by this activity. As Boo began to drink his red juice she hit him in the chest with force "Stop shaking!" All he could do was cry; nothing would calm this shaking. I still see the tears rolling down his face like it was yesterday. After Boo was hit, my mom was calm when she spoke, "Just go and lay down." Whenever Boo was sick, we all slept in the same room together.

I went to bed and what I remember is what my sister told me about what happened while I was asleep. During the middle of the night Boo had awakened and had to use the restroom. He woke my sister up who had to take him. He passed out and ended up going to the bathroom all over himself. My sister undressed him and put his clothes in the washing machine. He was making grunting noises as if he was in pain. She was shaking him and trying to wake him up. He must have shown some sign of life and came to because he was sent back to bed. Ten minutes later, he jumped up again to go to the bathroom and passed out a second time. Again, he went to the bathroom all over himself. Again he was grunting and making noises as if he was in pain. My sister and Ozzie were shaking him and trying to get him to come to but this time, to no avail.

The ambulance was called. My sister said as she watched him, she could see his stomach rise and get really big and immediately flatten as if he were taking big breaths. The emergency medical team tried to get his mouth open but his teeth were clamped together. By the time my mom left to go to the hospital with Boo, my sister had awakened Nathan and me. His pediatrician Dr. Phoebus whom he loved so very much was on call that night. I remember being asked what my brother had eaten at school because of poison that was found in his blood. I was afraid, I just wanted my brother to be ok. I knew this was going to be the normal hospital stay and he would come back to us.

Friday, February 13, 1987

We were waiting on someone to give us a report of how our brother was doing. Ozzie had gone to the hospital to be with my mom and brother. When the door opened the three of us were in our room as we were supposed to be but we rushed downstairs. I stood on the steps, Nathan was in front of me and my sister was on the first level in front of the door. With excitement, fear and anticipation, we all asked in unison almost, "How's Boo?"

"Where's Boo?"

My mom, aunt Ozzie, and my mom's two friends from high school walked through the door. Again we asked, "Where's Boo?"

My mom said in a calm voice, "Boo died."

You mean like never coming back? He died as in really died? He died as in I will never see him again? All of these questions were racing through my mind. I had never experienced "THIS" type of death before; none of us did. I remember being at the funeral with my dad when his mom had passed, but I remember sitting on his lap and we played through the whole service. In my nine years of life I had not experienced a loss so great, so deep, and it hurt me physically, mentally, and emotionally. Everything in my body in that moment was hurting.

My sister was crying and screaming all over the floor, Nathan was in front of me in shock mode crying. Then there was me. I wanted to cry, scream and kick but I just couldn't. So many questions flooded my mind. Someone had to show a sign of strength. I made myself hold back the thousands of tears that wanted to flow. I wanted everyone to know that I was strong and could handle it. I was at that moment in the words of Tupac Shakur "dying inside, but outside looking fearless." The truth is, I really couldn't handle it. I had just lost my best friend. He was almost my twin. I had just lost the one person who knew ALL of my childhood secrets and I knew his. My brother knew me better than anyone else in the world.

I had so many questions in my mind. *Who is going to finish teaching me how to ride a bike? Who will I walk to the bus stop with in the mornings and after school? Who am I going to graduate from the fifth grade with, then middle school and high school? We were in the same grade, the same school, the same teachers, but who would be there now? Who would be there at school to look out for me now?* My true sense of security and safety left me when Boo died.

I held in all of my tears. The whole time, my face was throbbing and hurting holding back my emotions. I wanted to be right with my sister kicking and screaming. She completely lost it. Ozzie turned to her and said, "Calm down, just because you lost your brother doesn't mean you can't get you're a** beat." Then she turned to me and said, "Good job you're the strong one. You didn't cry." Couldn't she see in my face how badly I was hurting? There were no hugs, no nothing; we were acting like Boo just hadn't died.

Later that day, mom called the school and gave them the news about Boo. I was wondering how the teachers were reacting. I wondered what some of them would say, would they cry too? Did they love us? Would they miss him like I already missed him, so much? The rest of the day is a blur but the next morning my siblings and I were in the kitchen with my mom and we had to be quiet so we would not wake up Ozzie. I could tell that my mom was hurting and in that moment, it hit me and I broke down crying. I couldn't hold it any longer. I missed Boo too much and death became a reality to me. I didn't like it. There was nothing I could have done to stop it. I hated death but I was also afraid of it. Death had taken one of the most important people in my life.

I climbed under the table and cried. My mom was there, she told me it was ok. My brother and sister actually chuckled a bit because I had waited so long to cry. I knew that they were hurting and that they were actually laughing to keep from crying.

Family Reunion

After what seemed like decades, we were permitted to go and see my grandmother and her older sister, Aunt Sadie again because of what happened with Boo. We hadn't seen them in almost a year or two. My grandmother was the youngest of 18 children born in Eufaula, Alabama in 1933. By the time my grandmother was born, Aunt Sadie was grown. She always took the opportunity to take us to church when we were at my grandmother's house. She didn't force us to go and my brother went more than we did at one point.

He would leave the three of us behind to go to Central Baptist Church with Aunt Sadie on the Hill. Rev. Green was the pastor at the time. We had grown close with the leadership at Central Baptist Church. Rev. Green, Rev. Gordon and Ms. Claire. They loved us like we were their own children.

I felt a freedom riding the bus downtown to meet Aunt Sadie - we finally had a chance to get out of that house. Although it took my brother's passing, we were going to a safe place. When she saw us, she hugged us tightly and cried. I could feel Aunt Sadie's love. She would always buy us nice clothes, but they were to be worn for church only and the clothes stayed at her house.

Because it had been so long since my mom had spoken to them, we had the task of asking her for one of my brother's suits to bury him in. She agreed to give us his gray suit with barely visible thin stripes. It was a nice suit.

The days leading up to his viewing, we stayed with my grandmother. We finally got to see him at the first viewing on Sunday, February 15th. My mom had been there early and was there all day. That morning everything seemed so dark to me. Mom called and I asked her, "What does he look like? Is he ok?" She just told me that she had seen all of our teachers along with other staff at the school who sent lots of hugs and hellos to me. Before we hung up she said, "I will see you soon."

When it was time to see our beloved Boo, We went to West Funeral Home. Inside of the building was a strange aroma of cologne most funeral homes used at that time. I looked up and saw his name and the dates and times of his services on a gold plaque. After what seemed like a mile long walk I turned the corner, and there he was. I hadn't seen him in days. I couldn't believe that the Tuesday before he had kissed me on my cheek and now he was lying before me lifeless. I wasn't focused on who was there I just wanted to see Boo. As I walked up to the casket, I had emotions, but I remember the biggest one was fear. I feared death because it was staring me in the face. It was my first time laying eyes on a dead body. I got close too Boo. I touched his hands and they were hard and cold as they lay at his sides. I didn't like it one bit. It was painful, it was scary, and I just missed him. I wanted one more hug, one more moment with him. There was this huge hole in my heart, a void in my life that could never be filled again.

The all white casket had real brass trim. His gray suit looked nice on him but his head was swollen. I was not sure if it was swollen from hitting the wall after Ozzie hit him in the chest.

It was good to see my dad. I felt safe. I knew that Ozzie would not do anything to hurt us while he was there. I looked around and there were many people there who genuinely loved us and were grieving like we were. One particular cousin, Denise called us her kids. She was hurt that we had been taken away from the family and had to get together for a funeral. I know she wanted to kill Ozzie right there in the funeral home. My aunt Debbie came over to us, she was so happy to see us. I overheard many conversations that night about how people were mad at Ozzie and wondered how my mom could let this happen.

Last Goodbye

We said our last good bye to Boo on Tuesday, February 17, 1987. We rode in a gray limousine. I wondered why Ozzie was with us and my dad was in another car. My dad had not seen Boo for a while but he was his father. At the funeral home a long line of people were waiting to get inside. I was shocked and happy when I saw Mrs. Howard, the assistant principal, teachers and students from our school. Mrs. Howard knew all of the students by name. I got out of the car and waived to all of my friends.

Our family went inside and sat down in the front. My brother and I eventually sat with my dad a few rows back. There was a long processional line and it delayed the start of the funeral. Watching them close his casket was so hard. My Aunt Sadie flipped out and cried and hugged his lifeless body. We all loved him that much. Our Carmalt classmates walked pass the body and some were crying but everyone looked sad. A lady I had never met sang a slow rendition of "Precious Lord." My Aunt Debbie and her sister Darla also sang. That's all I remember.

We buried Wesley in Greenwood Cemetery. The drive there seemed like an eternity. The reality that he was buried in the children's section would not hit me until years later when I called the cemetery so that I could visit him. It didn't seem right. Why would a cemetery have a section for kids? Truthfully, it is real. Death has no age limit. After the funeral we returned to our normalcy.

My first day at school was the following Thursday. My friend Dara came to check on me because I forgot that every Thursday morning was our television program at the school. The students would record things and programs and our principal would allow them to be played after being edited. I was talking to Dara when the television in our classroom came on. I guess everyone knew about the special program for Boo except for me. I watched, and listened as our principal Mr. Wikovich talked about my brother and the great student and person that he was. He talked about some of the things he liked and some of his friends like Eddie Lewis, and he mentioned me. After the broadcast was over, his picture appeared on the screen with his birth date and death date.

I don't know when I started crying, but Dara put tissue in my hand and on my desk. Even in elementary school, she acted like a mother to me. I chuckle now thinking about how she tried to convince her mom and dad to adopt me.

OPEN DOORS

I was sitting in my fourth period, Mrs. Ferraro's science class when the Vice Principal requested that I go with her to the office. I was shocked and wondered why I needed to go to the office. I had never been in trouble at school; I had never even seen Mrs. Howard's office. I wondered if I was in trouble at home. Mrs. Howard didn't say a word as we walked to her office. When we got there, a lady was sitting there waiting already.

Mrs. Howard asked me, "How are you doing Qiana?" Mrs. Howard reassured me that I was safe and she stayed in the room with me the whole time.

"I'm ok." I didn't tell her I was so happy to be at school because earlier that morning the last thing I heard was that I was going to get beat when I got home for eating a piece of cake. I was afraid.

The woman introduced herself as Vicky Tushay. She wore glasses and had reddish brown hair. "I came to your school to talk to you about how you feel about things going on at your home. I work for an agency called Children and Youth Services, sometimes we are called CYS." Vicky had already been to see my sister that morning. She and Mrs. Howard continued to reassure me that I would be safe for telling the truth. I thought, to myself, *Well, it certainly can't get any worse.* I told everything. I talked about the beatings, not being able to eat, sleeping on the floor on a sheet and every thing else that had been happening to us. I was disclosing for myself, my siblings and especially for Boo Bear. No child should have to live like that.

After I answered all of her questions, the social worker asked the ultimate question that would rock the core and change the course of my life forever. "Would you like to go home?" I was shocked and even had to think about it. Of course I did not want to go back but I also did not know what was ahead.

"Where will I go?" I asked her, "What is the plan? If I say yes will I get in trouble for talking to you?"

After a long explanation of how it would not hurt me to leave, I had finally come to a conclusion that I was not going home. Once I had made the decision, the social worker told me, "I already spoke with your sister. Not only do your stories match, she too revealed that she does not want to go home." The social worker told me that she was going to talk to my brother and ask him the same thing. "Going home is your choice. If Nathan states that he wants to go home, I will just deal with you and your sister." Before she left she took pictures of the marks on my arms.

I prayed that he would say no. As I sit and write today, I ponder why we were ever given a choice to go home. We were beaten, to the point of black and blue marks. Who would give a kid a choice to go back to something like that? I was told to report to Mrs. Howard's office after last period and that is exactly what I did.

I came back to her office to wait on the social worker to pick me up. Mrs. Howard offered me some thin mint cookies. While I ate the cookies, she looked at me with her big beautiful eyes letting me know that everything was going to be fine. For one of the first times in a very long time, I felt safe. I was once again in the presence of an adult that would not hurt me, someone that I knew I could trust. When the social worker came to pick me up my brother was in the car with her. He too had told the truth and advised he did not want to go home. The social worker said that our stories matched. There was no doubt in my mind that we would all tell the same story. Now it was just a matter of all of us being together and being safe.

After they picked me up, we went to my sister's middle school to get her. I did not know where we were going, I did not know what was going to happen, I had never in my life heard of a child protection agency. To my surprise, we were dropped off with my dad. We hadn't seen him since my brother's funeral it was such a joy and a relief to see him and know we could be with him. The social worker met my dad at his aunt's house, his mother's only sister. Although the cousins were older and my dad's age, we always had a great time when we saw them. It was not your average family, but it was family.

One thing that I came to realize as an adult that I could not possibly fathom as a child was that the agency placed us with my dad and he did not have his own home. Although I loved him very much and there was no place in the world that I would have rather been than with my dad, he was living with friends and relatives moving from house to house. They took us from one environment of physical abuse and neglect and put us into an entirely different situation that was not the best choice for us either. He was a grown man without a place to stay who suddenly gained custody of three kids. The social worker never came in and looked around at the house to see it was safe or clean. No one ever questioned how many people were living in the house; we were simply dropped off.

We spent the night with our cousins in a three-bedroom apartment. We slept in the living room on the floor. Although it was not much better as far as living, it was great because I knew that we were safe. We were able to live like normal kids again. The next morning, we got up early and were taken to another relative's house; although I did not know them, they knew me. Most of our relatives were much older than my siblings and I.

108 Letsche Street

Upon arrival to this new home we walked in the door and down a long hallway. We went straight to the kitchen where our relative had breakfast ready for us. There was a woman standing at the sink who was affectionately known by that side of the family as "Grandma Bea." To others she was simply, Ms. Bea. She had a five-bedroom home where my older cousin, her husband and two children, along with Grandma Bea and her husband already lived. Nathan met her great grandson who was his age. They instantly connected and started playing together. Nathan was happy to have a playmate.

In the attic were two bedrooms. My siblings and I would share one bedroom and her husband stayed in the second bedroom. Her bedroom was on the second floor. My sister and I shared a bed and my brother had his own bed. A few days later, we had our first court hearing. I had not seen my mom since I had left for school the morning of our removal. Typical protocol for the first hearing is to make sure the adolescents have temporary shelter and custody for 30 days, and then there is a new court hearing. During that first hearing, my dad was awarded custody of us after the Judge heard our stories. My mom and Ozzie tried to convince the social worker and the courts that there was no abuse but that they disciplined us because we were bad.

After the court hearing, we went back to 108 Lestche Street. I had fun attending to my little cousin Nicole who we affectionately called "Sugeez." She was two years old. She called me her "Piana." My sister was a teenager and she had made friends in the neighborhood. She got a job with her friends running a paper route. After the court hearings were over, no one saw my dad after that for about eight months.

We would hear complaints from the adults about him not being there and needing to take care of his kids. Even though people said negative things about our situation, we persevered. People told me I would never become anything and at the time I believed them. Over time I learned to change my way of thinking which eventually changed the way I lived.

Our situation had gone from bad to worse. We were three kids, with no sense of guidance and no father around who were living with family members who had only seen us when I was a baby. My dad never called or came back. While my dad was away, my sister was almost raped by our cousin's family from their other side. I was ten years old trying to stabilize my life while taking care of my brother and myself. It was hard and I didn't know what to do. I didn't know how to do my hair, how to properly get my clothes out for school or how to wash clothes. This began a season of being teased because of the way that I looked. Yet, I am extremely grateful that they allowed us to stay.

Dad's House

When my dad finally came back I closer to the age of eleven and I was doing all that I could to make it. There had been no permanent female role model in my house. He explained to everyone that he had been incarcerated. A short time after he returned, he got a call that his apartment was ready and he took Nathan and I with him. My sister stayed with one of our neighbors who had a daughter that she was really close to. We moved into a project called Broadhead Manor. Two of our Aunties from Arlington Heights lived close to us in another project complex up the street. It was great to be around everyone again.

When we moved, my sister's guardian bought my brother and I beds. She was there when we moved into the apartment. She was really excited for us and was happy to help. After she left, it was just the three of us ready to start our new lives together. These beds would be the only furniture for a long time. We eventually over time got a chair, a couch and an old television in the living room. My dad worked at the Hilton Hotel.

One of my dad's best friends was a drug dealer in the city. He was what comedian's call an "old school player." The man was always dressed in a suit. He and my father would mix their cocaine and marijuana on the table and put them into tiny little bags. I didn't mind marijuana being around because it reminded me of when my dad would blow marijuana smoke in my brother's face to help with his pain.

I used to play outside all the time. Although I was only ten, I can remember being outside until almost 3 a.m. because I was bored one night. I knew that I wouldn't be locked out because the locks on the door were broken. The night air was beautiful - cool and breezy. I sat and chatted with close friends until it was time for them to go into the house. I stayed until my dad came and got me. One summer day, I had been outside playing and when I went into the house my dad was smoking something. I knew what it was but asked him anyway, "What is that?"

"It's a pipe. It's my father's day gift to myself so I am going to smoke it." Both of my parents had used drugs and there was nothing about their physical appearance that stuck out to make them look unusual. They were never "strung out." My dad was always a healthy size and my mom was a diva; she was always sharp. My mom actually used to have what they called a kit. It was a tiny golden spoon and a tiny gold container where cocaine was kept. My mom and Ozzie would use the small spoon to sniff it up their nose.

The apartments in Broadhead Manor had utility closets that were spacious enough for me to play in with my toys. I would go into those closets and play with my baby dolls or play dress up with some belongings that I had collected from my mom. When I was in there playing one time I saw bags full of long narrow clear objects; I opened up one of the bags and saw they were full of needles. I didn't know at the time if they were for medical use or for drug activity but I found out; they were for drugs. Thank God I was smart and cautious when I played around them.

A Break from Dad

After a few months of living with my father I moved back with my sister and our neighbor. The neighbor carried on the legacy that my great aunt had started by taking us to church. I loved going to church in Coraopolis, PA. The singing and the love from the members felt great to me. I remember the wonderful family dinners at her mother in law's house. This neighbor would take as many kids as she could to church. She loved everyone and had a smile that would brighten up a room. She talked to me about accepting the Lord into my life one day. It was during our drive back home from church one Sunday that we had an in depth conversation about Jesus Christ and what He did for us. I was intrigued. I wanted to go to heaven. I wanted to see my brother again, so before we went into the house I accepted the Lord Jesus Christ into my heart.

Although most things went well with the neighbor, I hated the beatings. It seemed as if I was the one chosen most to be paddled. She used a thick brown wooden paddle. Because of the beatings there, my stay only lasted a few months. I asked to go back with my dad. A few weeks later, a car pulled up and my sister moved back too.

All Together Again

We were all back with my dad. On a few occasions, the cops came to our house and arrested him. Once when they came and he wasn't there they searched the house and found a few small bags of marijuana in one of my coat pockets. They asked my siblings and I who the coat belonged to and we told them it was mine. They wanted to take my sister to jail, but because she was only sixteen they couldn't take her. If the coat had been hers, she would have been arrested.

GROWING UP

Things began to happen with my body. I started to pick up weight and my shape began to form. I was an eleven-year-old girl with a body I had no idea what to do with. Clothes were no longer fitting, shoes began to feel uncomfortable, and my shirts felt weird. No one had taught me about puberty. Thank God for commercials and common sense, I had started wearing bras and that took care of the funny feeling in my shirts.

All while this is going on, CYF had come back in the picture and we were removed from the home again. The court granted custody of my sister to a relative in New Jersey and she moved out of state. Nathan and I did not want to be separated so they contacted our cousin on Lestche Street who agreed to allow us to come back. She was in her seventies and was no help on the puberty dilemma, telling me "It has been too long for me. I don't remember those things."

After what seemed like an eternity of moving back and forth, we were in "somewhat" of a stable home with food, clothes, and shelter. We were safe from physical abuse yet verbal and mental abuse was still hell to pay. During our stay there, many things happened to me. I was approached by one of an adult cousin's husband while walking home from cheerleading practice. In order to get home, I had to pass their house. He was on the porch and called my name. He said that my cousin was inside and wanted to talk to me. I went upstairs and noticed that she wasn't there.

He offered, "Do you want something to drink?"

I declined and I was ready to leave. "You are so beautiful and thick." He was trying to touch me. It was a good thing that I stayed close to the door. I was able to get out and run home. When I got home, I told my guardian. She was furious and called my cousin. They came over to the house and we all had to sit in the kitchen and discuss the matter. I was hurt and surprised when my cousin suggested that I was making up the events and her husband was telling the truth. He told her that I came into the house on my own and that I came onto him. She suggested that I was fast and had always liked him. For starters I was not into anyone at the time. If I had been looking for a relationship, my first choice would not be a grown man with no teeth!

I share this to encourage all of you who are parents and guardians of pre-teen girls and boys to show them love. Educate them about their bodies. Be someone that they can trust and open up to. If they tell you that someone is touching them or has touched them, or is even trying to touch them, believe them. Communicate openly, listen as they speak without reacting, respond to what they tell you, and above all else, love them. In so many families when young people disclose molestation or abuse it is often swept under the rug, ignored, or not discussed at all. These perpetrators are not worth our young people's integrity, self-worth, or esteem. Situations like these cause wounds to fester. They are seeds planted that cause a root called promiscuity and homosexuality. If it's not addressed early, broken children become broken adults.

A Mother's Presence

My mom was somewhat in the picture. We would visit her some weekends. She had separated from Ozzie and had formed a relationship with another woman. This woman was actually Ozzie's best man in the wedding. She was much nicer than Ozzie. My brother and I would play with her grandkids on the weekends when we would visit.

One summer day after we had finished all of our chores we were relaxing in our rooms. My younger cousin was visiting and we were having a quiet day until the phone rang. Our mother would often call our guardian and start fights with our cousin because she was taking care of us. She would always threaten her and talk about how she wanted her children back. I guess my cousin was tired of the arguing because that day, my cousin hung up the phone and told my brother and I to pack our things because we had to go back and live with our mother. "I don't care about no court order, you have to go." Within an hour, my brother and I were driving back to be with our mom. We were both completely devastated. Although the situation at our house wasn't the best, it was better than where we had previously been. I encourage all parents, if you are in a situation and you know that you are not stable enough to take care of your kids, swallow your pride and do what is best for your children. I promise they will appreciate you for it later.

In an instant we went from having our own room to living in an extremely small two-bedroom house with five people in it. I slept in the living room on a couch bed, my brother shared a room with her girlfriend's adult son, and my mom and her friend had a room. A few weeks after we moved in, my grandmother had to move from Miller Street to live with us. Gram slept on the sofa bed with me. It was nice being with her, but it was still hell being with my mom. The only place that we loved to escape to when my brother was alive was gone. Grandma's landlord was older and her grown children sold the property to the city.

Grandma was always strong and independent. She was neat and organized, yet Grandma was stubborn. She did not want to leave her home with so many memories and so much history for us. Honestly, I couldn't blame her. My grandmother had all of our baby pictures, pictures of my mom, her graduation cap and gown, pictures of her brothers and sisters and her parents. She had the only copy left of my brother's obituary and kept it on her mantle along with our baby photos. We had to pack all of these things and put them into storage. My gram didn't want to leave that place. I felt her pain; I didn't want her to go either.

A few months later, we had to move again. I had no clue why. My grandmother went to New Jersey to be with her sister. The rest of us moved into a two-bedroom project with the daughter of my mom's girlfriend. We went from six people in a two-bedroom house, to twelve people in a cramped two-bedroom apartment in the projects with ages ranging from newborn to 60. I was starting my freshman year in high school and I was thirteen or fourteen. I had to catch two buses to school. I was glad when we left there and moved to Homewood.

The time I spent with my mom during those years she mostly yelled and degraded me. I wasn't allowed to use the phone to talk to friends. If she was generous, she would let me talk but gave me a two-minute time line. Whenever my two minutes were up, she would pick up a phone from another room and harshly tell me to get off of her phone. When I needed things she would tell me that she didn't have money. For some reason, she was always thinking that I wanted to fight her. She would always say, "If you think you're bad, do something." A threat of my life and what she would do with it always followed. There was no physical display of love, private girl time, no talks about the things that I had to deal with like peer pressure, self esteem, boys, why I was teased and talked about by other kids, and no one had talked to me about puberty!

Day Dreaming

I started day dreaming a lot when we were with my mother. I figured I could at least dream about the life that I wanted to be living to escape my reality. I was a sophomore at my second high school. We were living with our mom and visiting our cousin on Lestche Street on the weekends.

One weekend over there changed the course of our lives yet again. There was an activity at school that I really wanted to participate in. The cost I believe was about $20.00 per student. Of course I couldn't go: my mom didn't pay for anything. If there were things happening at school, I was not in attendance. As much as I wanted to participate in things like that, I couldn't. I was basically taking care of myself, teaching myself and building myself up. I got teased and talked about a lot.

Since we were going to our cousin's house that weekend I figured I would ask her or her husband for the money. I did and it backfired. She called my mom arguing and fussing because I had asked for money to do this activity at school. My cousin handed me the phone. As usual my mom screamed and cussed me out. She called me all kinds of names as she usually did. All I wanted to do was participate in something at school; I was fed up with that situation. I was not able to go to my eighth grade graduation. My freshman year was a bust due to constant moving and I was just done with it all.

While my mom was yelling over the phone she says, “I am going to f--- you up when you get home,” and hung up on me. I looked at my brother. He saw my face and knew that I was tired. I said to my brother I don't want to go back. He surprisingly said, “Me either.”

Running Away

“I’m not going. I'm running away.” Up until this point my

brother and I had never been separated. He agreed that he was coming with me. I called a cousin that we trusted would help us and told her everything. We had a plan of escape. We left Letsche Street that night and went to her house. When we got there she told us that she had informed another relative who was going to let us stay with them in West Mifflin.

That night was a long night. We didn't go to my mom's house and we didn't show up for school on Monday. The first few days went well. No one called or came looking for us. I called one of my close friends and told her where I was and that I was ok. I had sworn her to secrecy. My brother and I were laying low for about a week. One day someone I did not know from the neighborhood recognized us. "Are you the girl on television who is missing?" Up until then, no one knew that we had run away. All they knew was we were visiting our family and we all wanted to keep it that way. I told her that I wasn't missing.

She disagreed, "I just saw you and your brother on the news." We watched the news that night and saw our pictures. They were asking people for information on our whereabouts and stating the last place we had been seen. Seeing myself on the news brought back the memory of the tribute to Boo in elementary school.

The next morning, I got a phone call from my friend. She was at school in the office. Police and security guards had questioned if she knew where I was or if she had talked to me. She told me that she did not tell them where I was but she was calling me to prove that I was safe. The security guard at the school who knew all of the kids got on the phone. "How are you doing? I promise that you and your brother will be safe if you come home. There are a lot of law enforcement officers looking for you." He told us that if we didn't want to go back with my mom we didn't have to. "You and your brother need to come talk to me."

Between him, my friend, and my cousin, we agreed to do so.

The local police came and got us. They took us to the office of the police commander. To my surprise, she was an African American woman. She had a round face with gray hair. We sat down and she lit a cigarette. She began speaking directly to me. She was so kind and wonderful.

"Hi Qiana, my name is Commander Gwendolyn Elliott and we've been looking for you and your brother." She asked how we were doing. "What happened? Why did you decide to run away?" She reassured us that we were safe.

My brother and I told her everything from start to finish. As she listened and smoked her cigarette, she would nod as if she understood what we were trying to convey with our words. After we had finished telling our story, she told us that she was going to call our mom. "Are you ready?"

We told her we were ready and when Commander Elliott called our mom, she informed her that we had been found. My mom sounded happy on the phone and I could tell she was crying. "I am glad they are safe."

Commander Elliott asked the infamous question that we had been asked so many times before at this point, "Do you want to go back home?"

Our answer was the same as it had always been, "No."

Since we had been in the court system recently, commander Elliot got our cousin to take temporary custody of us until our hearing with family division court. Just like that, we were back out of my mom's house and living again in temporary foster care with a family member as our guardian. They granted them custody, but in all honesty, that was not the best place for us. To sum it up in one word: turmoil. All of our cousins are so much older than us. But it was not really my cousin's wife's fault. She did the best that she could to cope with the situation. Her heart was truly in the right place. She would help anybody that she could. I can't imagine trying to take on someone else's teenage children without any warning and having to deal with your own craziness at the same time. But again, this living situation was extremely hard for us.

The turmoil in the house was an attack on my character. I had been through everything under the sun at this point. At fifteen years old and going into the eleventh grade I was still trying to understand life, love, and my body. I had my first boyfriend at the time and he was a friend that I had known since the second grade. Having a boyfriend meant that we sat outside together and talked in front of the apartment where adults and everyone else could see us. We would hug or he would put his arm around my shoulders or waist when we talked. Sometimes he would give me a peck on the lips but that was pretty much the extent of our physical affection.

My male cousin saw me with my boyfriend and accused me of being fast and promiscuous. "You are going to end up pregnant at a young age." He was comparing me to his own children. In his mind, I was the complete opposite of the person that I truly was. To be honest, I wasn't thinking about sleeping with anyone. I had no clue about sex and what it really was. I only knew what I heard other people say about it, what was on television, or things that I had heard in school. From what I heard, I wanted no parts of sex.

Around this time, my sister came into town to try and get custody of Nathan and I. She was married and had two young children of her own. We were going back and forth to court. I was in my third high school by now. For some reason the court did not give my sister custody, let's just say it was for the best. She went back to New Jersey.

Angels Watching

While in this home I attended Morning Star Baptist Church. The Lord has been a constant on my journey. No matter what phase I was in even as a little girl, God would send what I now call my Angels here on earth to love me enough to keep the presence and love of God in my life. God always strategically placed "Angels" in my life to make sure that I had what I needed physically, spiritually, mentally and emotionally. They are crown jewels, my diamonds, because they each had a hand in helping me to wear my crown right.

One week the church brought in a preacher in the area who was known as a great revivalist to speak. The revivalist extended an altar call for those who wanted to come back to Christ as well as those who were hurting and needing prayer. I had already accepted Christ in my life when I was younger but sitting next to my cousin Dora I had a weird feeling. Butterflies were in my stomach, my heart started pounding, and my mind was racing. I wanted to go up for prayer but I just wasn't sure. I sat quietly with all of these things happening on the inside of me. Dora leaned over and said to me, "If you want to go up for prayer, I'll walk with you. Brace yourself because my mom is going to cry a lot. You already know how she is, but I got you." We chuckled and walked up together.

That moment changed everything in my life spiritually. I rededicated my life to God at the age of fifteen. I believe had I not said yes to God in that moment, I might be telling you a different story today. I felt peace. Soon after that, I started classes and was baptized at the church. I joined my cousin and her best friend in performing arts ministry.

Separated from my Brother

One night while practicing for a ministry event at her best friends house, we got a phone call. Her best friend looked at me and I knew something was wrong. She started using the initials to people's names that were involved in whatever she was talking about. After she hung up the phone, I asked what happened.

"Let's go, I think your family should tell you." We drove back to my house and my brother was nowhere to be found. I was told that some inappropriate things happened and my brother was involved. The police were called and he was taken to a juvenile detention center. This was the first time in our lives we had been separated. We always wanted to stay together no matter what. I prayed that nothing else bad would happen. When Nathan was released from the detention center he was sent with my mom. I stayed with my cousins.

Sweet Sixteen

On my birthday I wasn't expecting much because I knew I wasn't going to get much, if anything. But I was excited, as most teenagers are to reach the rite of passage age. I had been a pretty responsible teenager. I did what I was told, I asked permission, and I was always around people who were much older than me. My cousin and her best friend kept me out of trouble.

The day before my birthday my cousin's friend and I had planned to go to a mime rehearsal. I had cleared it with my guardian. She had plans that day and was completely fine with me going. I had done my chores and called her before I left to let her know that I was leaving as I was told. As I left the house, her husband, my dad's first cousin was watching me walk up the street from his bedroom window. He never took his eyes off of me. The walk to where I was going was two minutes.

Upon my arrival my guardian was on the phone yelling and screaming about how I had snuck out of the house. I was totally confused. I had just spoken to her. My confusion had grown to anger. This was not the first time something like this had happened with him. I had done nothing wrong. I had been penalized for him thinking that I was fast and being promiscuous. I was doing none of that. While she was on the phone screaming, I grew angrier. She said, "You are on punishment for a week and you can't go to mime practice. Go home." I couldn't believe it. Every birthday had been horrible, and now my sweet sixteenth would be ruined.

I never had a birthday party and I was not trying to be on punishment especially because an adult could not control his own mental insecurities and pride. I told her I did not want the punishment and I was not taking it. I tried to explain about my birthday and remind her of the conversation that we literally just had. She responded that she didn't care and if I didn't want to take the punishment I could leave. To be honest, she was screaming and frustrated because her husband had just been screaming at her. So, I politely said, "Okay." We hung up the phone I walked back to the house, grabbed a few things, got on the bus, and left never to look back even though I had nowhere to go.

The safest place for me to go was my aunt Shelia's house. She had a house full of people and was cooking dinner for a party but it was okay that I showed up unannounced. Anyone that knows my Aunt knows that she always had the best sound system, played the latest and greatest music, and gave awesome parties. I told her what happened. She was very concerned but wanted to do the right thing. She called my caseworker and the non-emergency police number. She found out the best solution for me. After she hung up, we ate dinner and talked until we needed to go outside to wait for the authorities. There were no flashing police lights and one cop car came to the house. My aunt spoke to the police in her own way, "I don't want no trouble or no harm to come to my niece." She made them promise that they would take care of me. I left when the social worker got there. By the time we got to the emergency shelter it was late. After my intake was done I was given blankets. I went into the activity room, found a couch and went to sleep.

The next morning, I remember opening my eyes while lying on my back. The reality of where I was and what happened hit me. I was in a new place, it was my sweet sixteenth birthday and I was waking up in an all female youth emergency shelter. The other girls were excited to see somebody new. (As I wrote this part I got a little choked up) I got up off of the couch, took a shower, changed my clothes and sat down to breakfast with the rest of the girls. Later on that day, the other girls in the shelter baked me a cake and sang “Happy Birthday” to me.

I had to have an emergency court hearing at family court. This time my temporary foster care was not family; it was a shelter. The judge postponed the hearing for thirty days, which was normal and I had to attend their school. This was my fourth school since starting high school and my second school in the eleventh grade. I was adjusting to my new life. The Judge extended my stay after the first thirty days. I was getting visits to see my mom and my brother on the weekends.

Peace at Home

A man from a place called Pressley Ridge told me that he was going to place me in a better setting because of my good attitude and behavior. I would still be in foster care, just with a foster parent and not in the emergency shelter/group home. The following week, I met one of my sweetest angels. When she came to pick me up, she was with her sister. The girls and I had snuck downstairs to see what she looked like. We made eye contact and she asked, “Are you Qiana?” I confirmed. She turned to her sister and said, "Look, she is so pretty.”

I left the shelter and moved in with her. I still call her my mom. For the first time in my life, I was truly at peace. When we got to the house, she showed me my room. It was awesome! It looked just like a teenager’s room should look. I had my own phone in my room. She cooked a big dinner that night, we talked and the night ended well.

My foster mom loved me beyond words. She treated me as if

I was her own child. I was allowed to go to the mall with my friends but I had a curfew. We talked about boys. I had a crush on a guy and when she found out who he was and saw what he looked like, she did not find him attractive. "He looks like a frog. You can do better." She treated me just like a mom should treat a daughter. The best part of it all, she was a former hairdresser and took care of my hair. To this day, I don't play when it comes to my hair. She showed me different techniques and how to do it myself.

Because I had moved around so much, I 've been blessed to know a lot of people in different areas around the city. She signed me up for the local school so I could continue my eleventh grade school year.

One of our favorite past times was watching movies. She had one movie that was actually a live concert by the hit gospel group The Winans. They were singing songs that I had never heard before. One phrase I remember them singing was, "It's gonna be alright..." Another song talked about not having to worry. My heart was pierced deeply by the lyrics and the music. I would watch the concert over and over. Sometimes while watching I would cry because the words were encouraging and I was reassured that God had been with me in my life. Hearing those words gave me peace that no matter what, it was really going to be alright.

My foster mom would sit with me and she would cry too. She would hug me and restate, "It really is going to be alright Qi." I took her words as confirmation. Sometimes we would pray and she would make me smile or laugh by commenting, "Isn't Marvin Winans cute?" He was the lead singer of the group.

After a while my mom wanted me to live with her. When it was time to leave my foster mother's home, I wasn't ready and neither was she. We wanted to stay together forever. We both cried all day like babies. We talked and had a really good conversation about the future. My biological mom had gotten a new apartment and wanted me to join her and my brother. The CYF system checked to make sure that everything was legitimate and the Judge granted that I go. We watched our favorite concert together the night before. After I left, for a little while she would still visit me. When she cooked some of my favorite meals, she would bring me plates of food. We loved one another dearly and still to this day, that same love remains.

Freedom

Going back home to my mom's was not too bad at first. The court told my mother that in order to have custody, she could not have anyone living in her home besides the three of us. Mom rented a nice apartment, bought food once a month and paid all the bills, but didn't stay in the house with us. She lived with her girlfriend. We cleaned, cooked, went to school and I had a job. We were permitted to have one or two close friends over for visits, but nothing major.

We eventually moved into another place so that my mom could be closer to us and stay with her girlfriend at the same time. I was buying my own clothes, shoes, and necessities. My mom forced me to pay her out of each paycheck and take care of my own needs. I was upset about that decision. When I became a senior in high school I went to the prom, graduated, and still kept my job throughout that time.

If I could go back as myself and talk to myself as a teenager I would teach myself how important it is to let go of all of the hurt bottled up inside. I would remind Qiana of her internal strength and would tell her that the most beautiful thing about loving herself is she is the one who defines it and no one else. Since I am a woman now, I say to myself, "Live, be Free."

As I was writing this chapter, a song by James Fortune played on the radio. The words that I heard in the song were, "Lord I trust you." Those words reminded me to keep trusting and believing in God, especially in my hardest places and my darkest hours.

Writing this book was not easy. But as I poured out my life in these pages, I didn't have a rock to physically stand on yet I trusted God. He always made a way. He always has and always will continue to keep me. He's always had my back. I have no choice, I trusted Him then and I trust him now.

I don't know which of my readers this pause in my journey is for, but I want you to be encouraged. You may be down but you are never out. Take it from me. It may not seem easy but then again, anything that's worth something never is. Keep pressing forward. Keep fighting for the promise and trust God.

Everything that you are going through is building your character and shaping who you are. I don't care what it looks like, you can and you will defeat the odds. You will win. Hold on and stand on God's promises. When you don't feel like you can stand any longer, stand some more. If you fall seven times get up eight. Someone is looking forward to hearing your story of success

A PLACE CALLED THERE

On June 14, 2013, an associate of mine preached a sermon titled, "A Place Called There." She referenced 1 Kings 17 and Jeremiah 23:11. She talked about the place where God told the prophet Elijah to hide himself by the brook. She also talked about the brook being an uncomfortable place. The word "brook" means to suffer, to tolerate, to bear, and to put up with something unpleasant. It was in that uncomfortable place that God had spoken to the prophet. Although unpleasant, it was in that place that God covered him, fed him, and restored him.

I remember my place called "there." It was in that place where I experienced some of the worst hurt for a length of time. Thankfully I have been loved and restored by God. I discovered my place called there at the age of fifteen. My cousin had heard about a production that was being put on by a local pastor and his church for young people. We auditioned and with much struggle, we were placed in the production. That is where I met my future pastor and church family.

This church was like no church we had ever seen. The youth were active, the music was awesome, and I could also understand

and relate to where the word came from as well as how it was being taught. My brother and I loved it. I remember the day we joined the church. The pastor conducted an altar call, "Does anyone want to become a member of the church?" My brother raised his hand and stood up. It was a complete surprise to me. I thought to myself, *If they can reach my brother in a way that no church has ever reached him, this must be the place for us.* I stood with him and we joined our new church home. In my heart, I was sure that it was a safe place that would protect us.

It never occurred to me that anyone else, especially from the house of the Lord would hurt me. *Surely, I will find love and peace.* I thought I would be able to finally open my heart to receive love as well as trust people.

The wake up call came quickly. I was completely wrong. Not only was this my place called "there," it was one of the most difficult places of my process. Now, I realize the reason it was the most difficult is because I expected something different from church people. The people of God are supposed to love you no matter what, right?

I can relate to the prophet Elijah. I was lonely, frustrated and hurting. Just like the rest of my life, it served it's purpose and has a great meaning in my process to create the diamond that I am today. It was a place of many tears. A battle ground where I had to literally fight mentally, emotionally, and spiritually for my life. At times, I would barely be floating to stay above ground.

The church experience tore me down in a way that is almost unexplainable. Church hurt was real for me. If the young people really knew what I had to go through and deal with, if anyone would have ever walked a mile in my shoes, they too would have shed the tears that I was shedding. As a matter of fact, some of them may not have made it.

If hurt people come to church then that makes the saying true "Hurt people hurt people." I am not making excuses for the church. We as believers are held to a higher standard, but we are human. Donnie McClurkin has a song about people who fall down and get back up. One thing to realize about church is, it's not the building that you go to every week. God's people are the church.

Although we are held to a higher standard, that does not make us exempt from sin. As a matter of fact we sin daily by our thoughts, our words, and our deeds. But, what I love is the fact that we have a redeemer, Jesus Christ who died on the cross thousands of years ago and shed his blood for the sins that we have already committed, the one's being committed, and even the ones that we have yet to commit. When Jesus was crucified, he had to bleed, to make atonement for our sins. Once he bled, the veil was torn. Symbolizing, that we now have access to the Father, to his throne, because of the blood.

All of my friends from the neighborhood and Nathan stopped going to the church. Was it that there was no authenticity? I don't know. All I know is, I stayed. I stayed and was talked about, laughed at, and drug through the mud all because of who I was, where I came from, and how I was brought up. I remember people saying that I was gay or going to be gay just because my mother was a lesbian. Truth be told, I always have and always will despise that lifestyle because of what I experienced. I do not have a problem with gay people. I love everyone with the love of God but the lifestyle itself is not for me.

In my place called "there" I was abandoned in my brokenness. People didn't know how to take me or even respond to me. I was told later that when people joined the church they were instructed not to talk to me. I spent all of my teenage and young adult years at the church. When I met my husband at the age of 26 and got married I left.

What I have experienced in the church family would make a person never want to return. I kept going back to church because of the God that I serve. My faith, hope, and trust are created by God. I don't trust in people more than I trust Him. I always knew that there had to be something better for me. I could not give up on God and I trusted only Him. I would not be able to tell you my story today had those things not happened to me.

I think about my place called "there" often. I dearly love my former pastor. He truly is a great man of God. What's funny is, I may see or hear from different church members from that time and they say the same thing to me. I hear things like, "Wow, you made it and you were the one that they said would never make it." Or, "You were the one everyone least expected to come out." Someone even said to me, "I know how badly the people at church treated you. I remember what they used to say about you but you came out on top."

I ran into one woman who said, "I know you want to gloat or go back and say, "look at me now."

Up until that point, I had never given a response to any of those comments. But when she put a physical reaction to it, I had to speak on it. I would NEVER, in a million years think or do something like that. I've never been that type of person. And truth be told, I have not made it. I mean, what is the definition of someone "making it"? To me, you are successful when you are able to be confident, believe in, and above all, love yourself the way that God intended. Success to me is being able to love others effectively by giving, sharing, and caring. It means I can look at my enemies and say without gloating, "Thank you for the push." Success is not what people think it is. No one has truly arrived. For those who wonder, I have never looked down at anyone in my past or even thought any ill will against people for hurting me. I have been angry but I thank God for healed wounds.

My place called there will always hold a special place in my life because at the same time that I was being ridiculed and mistreated at church I experienced a wonderful relationship with God. The hard place pushed me to go hard for God – I had no other choice. It was my place of growth in Christ. I had my first real encounter with the Holy Spirit in that place.

I remember it like it was yesterday. We had just gotten out of Sunday school. Everyone was preparing for service. Praise and Worship had begun and everyone was singing. This particular day I was up close near the front and as soon as worship began, we went into what I know now to be another level. It was beautiful. My Sunday school teacher began to worship and went up into a high praise like never before. When she went up, it was infectious. One by one, worship filled the air. The glory of God was in that place. No words can truly explain what took place that day. It was my first time being in church where the Holy Spirit took complete control. Rev. as we affectionately called him, couldn't and didn't preach a sermon. God did what He wanted to do. I can't describe the feeling. I never wanted church to end that day. I wanted to stay all day to soak up what I was feeling.

After the service was over people were standing around and talking, but I couldn't speak. My heart was pounding and there was a strange yet amazing feeling that I was experiencing. I wasn't sure if I was supposed to tell anyone. I was focused on the conversation in my flesh, but my spirit was doing leaps.

I'll never ever forget that church. The pastor was strict, but in such a great way. He taught his congregation how to be leaders. We were taught the importance of Sunday school and Bible study. I was taught what being a leader is all about. I was taught what coming into ministry was meant to be. We were taught as leaders to study, to be faithful and to be accountable. So yes, I went through hell and back, but spiritually it pushed me right into my destiny.

My place called there taught me what not to do. Everything that happened to me there I used as a stepping-stone. As a matter of fact, if it wasn't for my experience there I would not have been able to birth my scholarship program, "Gifts for Grads". I wish you could see the smile on my face as I write this and think to myself, "My pain truly did produce my purpose."

My life has never been “normal.” While others were enjoying teenage years, I was basically trying to survive in a place that simply would not accept me. I worked, went to school, went to church and that was it.

My senior year in high school was different. I had already been to my fifth high school. While dealing with the church hurt, I still also had to fight, deal with drama, foster care, homelessness, and family at home.

I graduated from high school when I was seventeen. I knew that I wanted to go to college but I didn't think that I could and I didn’t have any help. I didn't know what to do. I just knew that I had to work. When one of my closest friends graduated the year after me she encouraged me to apply for school and I got accepted. I was nervous and excited.

Whenever seniors graduated from high school, the church would give a huge token of love when they went to college. They were given the basic necessities needed for their dorm rooms. I asked about the school supplies and necessities. I was told to let the person in charge of getting the things know what I needed. She said, "Ok, let's pick a date and we can go shopping together." I was happy.

We went out and we began to select everything that I needed and more for my room. When we got to the register I was shocked that I had to pay the $200 total. Thank God for layaway, $200 was a lot of money for me as an eighteen year old to earn!

I wondered if the things I bought were going to be presented to me in front of the church like they were for others as a gift even though I paid. I wondered if I was going to get reimbursed but that didn't happen. I promised myself as I stood in that line to pay for my things that I would never let that happen to another graduate, ever. That is how Gifts for Grads was birthed. I started using my own money to bless high school graduates going to college by helping to get the necessities needed for them to start college without the stress of not knowing where it would come from.

During my tenure in my place called there, I felt like people never understood me; they couldn't. They never understood my heart, my tears, how I fight for my life, my struggle just to make it on a daily basis. I was so young with the world on my shoulders. Again, all I knew was work, church and school. I have been working since the age of fourteen. I figured if I stayed busy I could just focus on that, being busy. It wouldn't be until later in life that I would realize being busy and being productive are two very different things. During these times, my mom was constantly arguing with me. For some reason, it seemed as if people wanted me to be the villain that they created; not the Qiana that I truly was. I would give anyone the shirt off of my back but then was accused of buying friends. I couldn't win for losing in that place. I was accused of doing things that I never did.

In my place called "there" I felt the presence of God. Although I had already been abused physically, verbally, and emotionally in that place I felt persecuted.

By the brook in my place called there, not everyone was mean. There were some smiling in my face and stabbing me in my back but there was one particular person who came to the church that was different. Of course she had heard just like the others to stay away from me, but she didn't. In fact, she always smiled and always had a kind word to say to me. She didn't act like I was a poisonous person as the others did. There were times that I would try to give up and do things as a young adult that were completely out of my character and she would correct me in love and show me where I needed to be.

Pastor Freda Thorpe is known today as one of my Angels, one of my sheroes. She was like my oasis in the dessert. She didn't care about my past. She didn't care what I looked like or how I dressed. What mattered to her was the heart of this young girl who needed to be loved the right way. She never judged me because of what I had been through and she covered me in prayer. Pastor Freda loved me for me and showed it by what she did, not by what she said. That to me is authentic love.

Being in my place called there I like Elijah couldn't understand it. As a young person I was going through more than what probably most of the adults were facing. But again, I LOVE THAT PLACE and I'll never disregard my place called "there."

MEET THE MONSTER CALLED DOMESTIC VIOLENCE

A few friends and I have a private, closed group on social media where we "Define our Greatness." In the group we discuss many political and diverse subjects. One of the recent topics of discussion was Domestic Violence. Up until that day I had no intentions of exposing that part of my journey. Here is a list of questions that were posed on that thread:

- Has anyone ever been in a domestic violence situation?
- Why did you stay?
- What made you stay after the first hit?
- What did we do to get out?

To my surprise, many women in the group answered affirmatively that they were survivors of domestic violence and began to tell their story. Many of them had been in cycles of leaving one bad relationship and exchanging it for another one. There were women who wondered why they attracted certain individuals into their lives. I knew that I had attracted who I was into my life.

My mother's lover was my abuser – a man had never abused

me. My father has only hit me one time in my entire life. Growing up I had experienced so much heartbreak, so much rejection, conditional, and fake love that I was not used to real love and could not find myself drawn to it. The most intriguing part of my experience is that I did not know what domestic violence was, nor did I realize that I was in a bad relationship at first.

Meeting the Monster

When I met my abuser, I was taking evening classes with a goal of making some awesome changes in my life. I started on the first day of English class ready and focused. English is one of my favorite subjects. When I got to class, my friend Dara from elementary school was the lone familiar face. We had kept in touch and talked often throughout the years. She and I are still extremely close today. I swear she acts like she is my mom. I love her for a lot of reasons but because she always wanted to protect me, I am grateful. Our routine every week was that Dara and I would talk, walk to our bus stops together and head home.

During one class the professor started a discussion about God and if He is real. We were comparing God to mythology. Well, I love open discussion so I was engaged in the conversation on "Team God is real." Our professor loved it. After class was over, someone came up to me and told me, "I enjoyed the way that you stood up for God." He started to say things that men often say when they approach a woman that they are interested in dating. He told me I was beautiful and that he liked my smile.

Until that point in my life a man had not approached me in this way. I was young and inexperienced and I thought he was a Christian, which was a plus for me. "What church do you attend? What do you do in ministry?"

I was so excited to finally feel like my thoughts were important. Someone was finally interested in what I did, and what I thought. Dara came over to see if I was ready to leave. I introduced her to him and she saw right through him. While giving me the side eye she greeted him, "Hello."

I just thought she was being her over protective self. I guess in a sense, she was. We all walked out of class together. He and I got on the bus together, we laughed and talked the whole time. That bus ride changed the entire dynamic of our relationship. We discovered that we lived close to one another and we started dating shortly after that class. We started traveling to school together. We shared textbooks, and did a lot of things together.

Everything seemed fine until the day we were at his apartment eating dinner and he said, "I have something to tell you." He reassured me that what he was about to say had nothing to do with us. "I care a great deal for you. This is why I need to tell you this. I want to be open and honest." He went on to explain that he would soon be placed on house arrest for a situation that happened between him and two other females while at a previous college. "The girls accused me of sexual assault but I am innocent. What happened was consensual. I fought the case, which is the reason why I was not convicted." He reasoned with me that to be fair the judge gave him house arrest and parole for a specific amount of time. "There was an altercation but nothing at all for what I am being blamed for."

That should have been red flag number one for me. But me being naive at the time, and not to mention that I have a gigantic heart, I told him, "It is okay. I will be with you and help you through the process." His house arrest restricted us from hanging out as much. He was allowed to attend his classes.

Red Flags

I couldn't dare tell Dara about the house arrest situation right away, she would have really gone off on me. She would openly confess that she did not like him. There was something about his demeanor that did not sit right with her. She would always say about him, "There is something about him that I don't like. Why are you with him?"

As time went on, he became more and more possessive and aggressive towards me. I was still active in church and we had gone together a few times. He attended his own church as well. During this particular time, our church was in the midst of convocation. Because I was in different axillaries and leadership, we were required to be in specific places at specific times while attending convocation. The young man had gotten angry because he couldn't see me as often or see what I was doing. "We have one more day of church convocation left. I will come and see you after church tomorrow."

We were in church for a long time that particular night and by the time I got to my apartment I was exhausted. Although eager to lie down and get some rest I checked the caller ID and noticed that I had missed several calls from the young man. As I was resting he called again. When I answered the phone he started an argument. "I missed you."

"I will see you tomorrow. I am really tired." I tried to explain what I had done that day at church to justify my exhaustion to him. "Besides, I don't have a way to get to you at this late hour."

"I already hooked up a ride for you to get here." He kept nagging and nagging, and I finally gave in. I didn't know why at the time, but I made sure to ask him if this friend who was picking me up would be there with us. For some reason, I didn't want to be alone with him. I would have felt more comfortable if someone was with us. He assured me that his friend would stay. Being that it was already late, I gathered my things for church in the morning just in case. His friend arrived at my place to pick me up. When we got to the apartment, his friend let me walk through the door first.

I thought he was being a gentleman but I misjudged the action. My abuser thanked his friend and shut the door behind me. To me he said, "I can't let you go home tonight." His tone and statement scared me. I didn't know what to think, so I played it cool like everything was fine.

I had just gotten my hair done and I had on new clothes. I slowly sat down at the table near the door with all of my things still in my arms. I kept hearing a weird noise. My abuser was behind me. I went to turn around to see what the noise was and he spit on me, in my face and in my hair. I got up to leave and that's when he hit me and again said, "You aren't going anywhere."

That was the first time I had been hit by a man. Of all of the abuse I had endured, no man had ever laid his hands on me. My father had never hit me like that. I questioned myself, *Is this the same Man of God I have been dating all this time? Is this the same man I thought was handsome and sweet?* He sure was.

I argued back and tried to push him away but he was strong and heavy. I tried to get over to the phone but he kept pushing me, and spitting on me, and taunting me. There was a small drop of blood on my dress. I knew my mouth was bleeding from the hit. I kept trying hard and he was grabbing and pushing and squeezing harder. So, I finally stopped. I just started to cry. He paused as if he felt bad for me. He grabbed the phone and said, "Here, call a ride so that you can go".

I believed him. I wiped everything off of my face, got up to get the phone, and he punched me again. Because I was already standing up he forced me into his bathroom. This was the place where he thought he could do what he was best at, abusing women. In the bathroom he thought the sounds would be silenced and no one could hear anything. In other rooms of the apartment building people may have been able to hear my screams.

He grabbed my hair and while tightening his fist he began to smack me in my face, and then he slammed me to the floor in a small corner between the sink and the wall. I was sore, out of breath, and my lip was a puffy and soft. I gave in. I was tired of fighting. He said it again, "I can't let you leave and by the way, I have to sleep with you tonight." I looked at him like he was crazy, but I knew whether I would allow him to or not, he was going to do whatever he wanted.

I was forced to stay with him for three months. I no longer wanted to be with him. I had to quit my job. It was the worst 3 months of my life. I remember telling his sister who couldn't help herself let alone help me. She would sometimes laugh at me along with him. If we left the house, we left together. I remember one time he was hitting me and spitting on me in public with lots of people around. No one said anything. No one spoke up or helped. I was surprised. I just figured it was fine. I had never experienced it, but society was definitely okay with it, at least that is what I was thinking at the time. He would always say how sorry he was and just do it again. Over and over, the punches in the face, a forceful kick in the stomach, the yanking and pulling of my hair; He would laugh at me, and call me names.

One day, I had a scheduled gynecological appointment. When my doctor was done, she left the room and closed the door. I love to read, so as I was getting dressed I began to read a sign on the back of the door. It was 10 questions about your relationship. I answered yes to every single question. When I got to the bottom, the statement read, "If you answered yes to at least one of these questions you are in an abusive or domestic violence situation." I was shocked. I had never really paid attention to the words "domestic violence" before. The poster said to tell someone and get out of it.

I left out of my doctor's office with a sense of awareness. I had to get out. When, I didn't know. How, I didn't know. I still had my own apartment but I hadn't seen it in so long. How would or could I get there without him knowing. I was determined to get out and I wanted to go home. I figured I could call my male cousins to rescue me. I was wrong. The response that I got was, "You'll probably go back to him anyway." I thought to myself, *who would want to come back to this?*

I continued to work on my plan and he continued to beat me. One day I had an intense feeling of courage that I had never experienced and it made me even more determined to get out. It was around 7pm. The last bus came at 9:50, so I had to think fast. I didn't care how, but I knew that I would be on that bus. My abuser started his usual arguing and slapping me. When he punched me in my face and my nose started to bleed I started crying. For whatever reason, that caused him to stop hitting me. His countenance changed to nice for some strange reason.

"I want to call my friend. He's like a big brother to me." My friend was a preacher. "He has known me since I was ten years old." My friend stood at 6'4 and was well over 200 pounds. I convinced my abuser to let me call just so that he and his wife would know that I was ok. To my surprise, he agreed. He went to cook dinner while I made my call. I spoke in code to tell him all that I had been going through for the past several months. He began to minister to me in love.

I could tell he was getting upset. "I could drive all the way across town and beat him to a pulp, but what would that prove?" He told me, "You really have to want to get out."

I didn't understand then why people kept saying things like that as if I would go back to the relationship. Once I was out, I was out. There was no going back for me. It wasn't until after I found that women tend to go back to their abuser in these situations. " God really wants to heal you and your abuser as well, however you really need to get out."

I was waiting for him to say that he was going to come and get me, and he didn't. He said, "If you really want to get out, I want you to get by yourself, and begin to pray. If you call on the name of Jesus, He will deliver you. "Although it was not the response I was looking for, I did just that. I got up and told my abuser that I was taking the phone into a different room to pray. He brushed me off, something that he would never usually do. I went into that room and cried out to God like never before. I cried so loud until I couldn't cry anymore. Then I just began to scream the name Jesus. After I was done, my brother prayed for me. After he prayed, he said, "Now get up, go home and call me when you get there."

I got nervous for a second. How was I going to explain to my abuser what had just happened let alone leave the house? He started knocking on the door. "I've been listening to you pray. Are you okay?"

I opened the door and told him, "I am fine." He had this weird yet scared look on his face.

He said, "I heard you calling Jesus, are you okay?" I reassured him that I was fine. He was being extremely nice. But his boldness quickly kicked in again. I knew I had to play it safe.

After dinner I said to him in a sweet voice, "My brother wanted me to go to church with him, his wife, and the family tomorrow. I agree that I need to go." He was quiet so I kept talking, "It is important since I haven't seen them."

To my surprise, my abuser agreed. "You can go home for one night. Leave your books and those work papers. I know you just got a job and you will have to come back."

I didn't care. All I cared about was getting out of that house. I would figure out a way to get my things once I had gotten out. I grabbed my keys to my house, he kissed me and I left.

I couldn't make it up that hill fast enough. I literally made it just in time for the last bus. When I got to my apartment, I had the weirdest feeling. I thought I was never going to see my place again. I locked the door and my windows. I was shaking but relieved to be back home. I just began to thank God. I immediately called my brother who was happy to hear that I was home. He told me to meet him and his family after church in the morning and to pack a bag because they were taking a trip to Ohio for a few days and I would be with them. After I hung up the phone with my brother, my phone rang again. It was my abuser. I answered and told him that I was home safe and going to sleep. I hung up the phone with no intention to ever speaking with him again.

The trip to Ohio was calm. It was a nice getaway from the world. I got home later that week feeling refreshed and happy. As soon as I opened my door, my phone was ringing. It kept ringing off the hook. I checked my caller ID. My abuser had called me over 50 times. I answered the phone. He started going off. "Where were you? Who were you with? Why haven't you called me?" He was getting irate.

"It's over, don't ever call me again. Good-bye." I hung up on him. He continued to call back leaving threatening messages on my answering machine. I was free from him. I was moving forward never to look back.

I went back to class that week knowing he would be there. I went early to let my professor and the security guard know what had happened. I told Dara who as I suspected was upset. "I told you I didn't like him."

Everyone worked together to keep me safe. I was able to be in class and take my tests in another location. He tried to talk to me, but the guard would not let him near me.

I knew that I had to get my things from his house so I called a friend and asked her if she would go with me. She agreed to go and we took her boyfriend along for the ride. I called his house and his mom answered the phone. I had seen him shove his mom before. "I want to get my things from over there. Will you be at the apartment to give them to me?"

She gave me a really hard time, but obliged. When my friend and I got to the house we knocked on the door and his mom cracked the door open and handed me my books. "For anything else, you will have to come back."

I knew he was there and the only reason he was not giving up my ID and my work papers was because he wanted me to come back alone. His mom insisted that he was not there. "I can't let you in the house unless he is here."

That weekend I decided to go to church. I had not been for a while and I was excited to see some of my friends. One of my male friends offered to give me a ride to the service. We had never been alone but we were all good friends and I had never felt any bad vibes from him. When he picked me up he surprised me when he said, "I need to stop by my house and grab something for church."

I didn't think anything of it so I went in with him thinking we would be there for a few minutes. I knew we were not far from the church. While there, he tried to rape me. I fought him off and ran out of the house. I found my way to my mother's house and I was traumatized. After everything that I had been through, this had to happen too? As I sat at my mom's house, I tried to get my mind together. This was a lot to process about myself and what I was experiencing.

I never made it to church that day.

Years later it was discovered that he was doing that to several women in the church and the Bishop kicked him out of the congregation.

I stayed the rest of the weekend at my mom's. I did some laundry and tried to get prepared for the week but I needed my things from the abuser's house. I called him. "I need to get the rest of my things. I need to start work this week." I heard a lot of people in the background. "I will come over but I will not be in your house alone."

"I am over us. You can come get it now." It was daylight and there were plenty of buses so I agreed. After speaking with his sister and his niece I agreed to go to the house. They reassured that they would be there and that nothing would happen to me. I believed them and so I went back.

When I got to the complex, I saw his sister's car and that relieved me. I got upstairs to the apartment, and to my surprise, the only person there with him was his mother. His sister had left and the car that I saw in the parking lot was not hers. As soon as I knocked on the door, he swung it open forcefully put his mother out and locked it behind us. He started talking to me. "You thought you were going to get away from me." Out of nowhere he just start pounding on my body. I was a little dazed, but I managed to remain standing up. He made me take off all of my clothes and put on nothing but his t-shirt, which was already folded up on the table waiting for me.

After I put the shirt on, he started screaming and yelling and hitting me. He made me go into the bedroom. "I want to know everything that you have done since the last time I saw you. Start from the beginning." He just knew that I was with somebody else and that made him angry. He made me walk in front of him and hit me from behind as I went into the room.

I began to tell my story and he cut me off, "Pause." He got up and went into the bathroom. He came back with a lit cigarette. As I began to finish, he began to burn me all over my hands, neck, and arms with the cigarette. Then he started punching and kicking me again and it felt like forever. When he stopped hitting me he barked at me, "Go into the bathroom."

I complied with his demands. While in the bathroom he burned me again, scratched my face and choked me. He stuck his fingernails deeply into my neck causing me to bleed. I started screaming. "Get off of me!" My screams fell on deaf ears. He burned me again, and because I was screaming, he took a cup that was sitting on the sink in his bathroom and threw the contents in my face. He had urine in the cup and it burned because of the open wounds on my skin.

He pushed me back into the bedroom. "Finish your story because I know that there is more." Before I sat down, he began kicking me. I was at this point sore and tired; I couldn't fight him anymore. I began to finish my story. I told him about the young man from church who had tried to rape me and that set him off into a fit of rage. "I knew you were with someone else!" He jumped up and started to punch me again. He grabbed me by my hair and made me go back into the bathroom. This time, he took a thick wooden brush and started hitting me over my head with it. That was pain like I had never known. It was fierce and it was piercing. As he was hitting me and yelling at the same time, I started to get dizzy, I thought to myself, *If you don't try and get out, he is going to kill you today.*

I reached up and started grabbing for the brush. My head was down so I couldn't see. I then tried to swing. I was tired and limp, but I was determined to make it. My hand hit the rack in the bathroom that towels are hung on and it broke on one side, so I tried to grab it to start hitting him. Somehow, when that happened the brush hit the floor, he started laughing and said to me, I will just use the metal rack on you. By this time we were both out of breath and I was tired. I had all of a sudden gotten really hot. I was breathing heavily and what I thought was sweat had started dripping down all over my face, my neck and the shirt. I just started crying out to him, "Please just stop." The sweat kept coming and I wiped my forehead and face. But as I looked at my hands, they were covered in blood.

There was so much blood that it scared both of us. The t-shirt was drenched in blood from my head. "Take it off." He gave me another shirt to wear. He began to clean up the blood and ran water in the bathtub and told me to get in it. I was still dizzy. I got in the tub and he got in with me. From behind, he began to choke me and tried to put me to sleep, thank God, it didn't work. He just looked at me, and I guess he thought, that was enough.

No More Beatings

I had endured several hours of abuse that night. As dizzy and tired as I was, I was still thinking, *I have to get out of here. God help me get out of here.* Then something happened. He started being nice again. The same kind of nice that he had become the last time I was able to get out. I didn't know why and I didn't care why, I was done. He looked at me and went to get a cigarette and realized he was out of them. He couldn't go out because he was on house arrest. So he looked at me and asked if I would go to the store for him. I happily agreed. That was my way out.

I quickly and carefully put my clothes on and asked if he needed anything else. I was so sore, but I didn't care, if it took my last breath, I was getting out of there. He gave me money and I left. On my way to the elevators, I looked over at the trash heap and saw he had thrown the bloody t-shirt and rags away. I was so dazed that I don't even remember him going out the door. It could have been when he told me to get in the tub.

A small convenience store was about a block away from his apartment. It was dark outside and very late at night. My plan was to ask the owner if I could use his phone to call my mom. The owner had seen me in the store with my abuser and I hoped he would recognize me. I was so happy to see the manager. He and a lady were in the front behind the counter. I mustered up enough strength and said hello,

I was about to ask if I could use the phone, but the manager interrupted me and asked. "Were you in a fight"? I didn't answer. He asked again, "Were you in a fight, with a man"? That question was followed by, "Did that guy put his hands on you? I never liked him. I knew he was bad." Everything he said from that point was muffled to me. I started to cry. He got the phone and said, "Call whomever you like. Make as many calls as you like. I am not letting you leave my store until someone that I know and trust comes to get you."

I called my mom. "I got in a fight and I need someone to come get me."

The store manager took the phone from me and when they hung up he said, "Your uncles are coming to get you."

I was relieved and thanked God aloud. My mom's friends lived close by and were at the store in a few minutes. I had only been gone for about fifteen minutes but it was too long for him. When he saw me walking to the car with the two gentleman, he ran up the hill toward me and began to plead and beg for us to come to the house and talk. "Don't leave Qiana." He must have called his parole officer and reported an emergency because he was not supposed to be outside of the house.

One of the gentlemen recognized him and asked him, "Who is your mother?" Ironically, they were related and the man was furious. He barked at my abuser, "I can't believe you are doing things like this! Does your mother know you are treating women like this? I am, going to make sure she finds out!"

We all went back to the house and his mom is there. I barely remember the conversation, I was extremely sore, dazed and tired, and I wanted to lie down. I must have dozed, I heard one of the gentlemen calling my name, "Qiana, he wants to talk to you in private." They gave him instructions before we left the room, "You can talk to her but leave every door in the apartment open."

He took me into the bathroom and he started kissing me. "Will you stay with me? Please don't leave me again." I barely comprehended anything at this time. I looked at him wondering why he wanted me to stay. I heard a call from the other room saying that our time alone was up. The gentlemen asked if I wanted to stay with him, I declined. "Get everything that belongs to you." I grabbed all of my papers and left.

Instead of driving me to my mom's house first, they drove me to the emergency room. It hurt to lie down, my head was pounding. I told the nurse that I needed to use the restroom. When I did, I finally got to look in the mirror to see what everyone else was seeing. I had a lot of blood in my hair. There were knots across my forehead. My hands and fingers were swollen with knots. My arms were swollen and red from the cigarette burns that had blistered. My stomach and sides hurt from him kicking me. My neck was bloody from when he tried to put his nails into it. My lip was busted. I was a mess.

The doctor ordered an MRI. While going into the machine, I had a flashback and went into a state of shock. The nurses asked me to be still and reassured that everything was ok. They sent me back to my room and a social worker for domestic violence came to talk to me. I didn't want to talk about what happened. I was determined not to go back to that man or to that place.

The nurse came in and said, "We have to keep you overnight for observation." I was terrified. I didn't want to stay over night. I was scared that my abuser would show up and start beating me because I didn't choose him that night.

I cried and begged, "Please let me go home to my mom's house. I will do whatever it was that you need me to do but please let me go home." The doctor was begging me to stay and I was begging to go home.

His voice was strong and his tone was stern, "I can't hold you here against your wishes. I need you to promise me that you will listen to my orders. It is detrimental that you do what I tell you to do. " His voice was calm and full of concern, "You seem like a responsible person and I trust that you will get better. Listen carefully and obey my orders."

It was weird that he kept telling me to obey but I listened.

"If your pain increases, come immediately back to the ER. If your headache is not gone within the next 12 hours, get back to the ER. If you sneeze get back to the ER. Do not move your head or neck at all. I need for you to lie completely still. Go to a place where you can recuperate well and in peace. If you get angry or excited, come back in immediately. No stress, and no movement, just rest."

"I promise I will do what you ask."

"Okay. I will write you some prescriptions and send the nurse back in with your release papers."

When the nurse came in with all of my instructions I asked her, "Why is the doctor so concerned? Why can't I sneeze?"

"Your brain is jiggled. We are all concerned."

"What do you mean my brain is jiggled?"

"Have you ever seen how gelatin wiggles back and forth? That is what your brain is doing."

I was sent home in a cab with pain meds and a weird looking

cushion to rest my head and neck. I was able to stay at my mom's house on her couch. She felt so sorry for me. She set up her living room for me like a mini hospital room. We took pictures of all of my wounds. My dad had sent his friends who were local police officers to talk to me. I learned that because the incident happened in a municipality, I had to go back to that area to file the police report. I couldn't let him get away with this. I was in so much pain that I had to file the report two weeks later.

At the police station I was informed that not only was my abuser on house arrest, but he was on probation for sexually assaulting another woman. I was shocked that the police officer had no compassion for me. "Well, you women always go back to the guy. We can bring him in for simple assault." I didn't care what they brought him in on; I was not going to let him get away with what he did to me. The cop started talking again, "It can take up to a year and the court hearings will get postponed." I had plans to follow this thing through no matter how long it was going to take. "We will go arrest him and you will get information about the preliminary hearing."

God's Grace

The preliminary hearing determines if a case goes to trial or the charges will be dropped. The day of our hearing was first time I saw my abuser since that night my Godfathers came to get me. His mother, sister and niece were all there, ready to testify on his behalf. The DA told me that he was pleading not guilty and that he only hit me because I was hitting him. He was basically just trying to defend himself. I still had marks on me from the cigarette burns. I still to this day have a slight dent in my head because of those hits with the wooden brush.

I thought to myself, *Of course I hit him back, I had to at least try and defend myself.* He had initiated every incident. I understood why those girls from his previous college had pressed charges on him. I believe that he forcefully sexually assaulted those girls and got off with lighter charges because he played innocent.

The Monster is Caged

Everyone including his defense lawyer was so shocked that I was going through with pressing charges against him. I was the only witness called to the stand. I had to testify and tell everything that happened that night. The defense lawyer tried to make it seem as if I was lying but was speechless when I answered correctly. My story never changed, how could it, it was the truth. After my testimony, the judge asked a few questions, looked at some papers and ordered the case to stand trial and remanded him to prison. I was relieved that he was going to be in jail but his family was hurt. I walked out of the courtroom knowing I had done the right thing.

The hearing was postponed several times. It took up to a year and I was not backing down. My abuser's lawyer finally convinced him to take a plea deal and he agreed. He was to pay a total of $5,000 restitution, which was the cost of my medical bills for the night of the incident. He was ordered to go through therapy and a whole bunch of other things. I was glad that it was over and I would never be in his presence like that again.

I saw him on the bus with another girl a few months after he got out of jail. The girl was much younger than me. She seemed happy, just like I was in the beginning. I wanted to tell her to run and get out while she could. When he saw me, he gave me an evil grimace to try and scare me. I looked him in the eye to show him that I was not bothered. I was no longer afraid of him and I was free of him.

Several years later I was awakened by a call from my best friend in the early morning. When I answered the phone her question woke me up immediately, "What was that guy's name that abused you?"

I confirmed his name. She screeched, "Oh My God, Qiana turn on the news, that's him!" I sat at the edge of my bed and turned on the news. He was the subject of breaking news and live coverage. The man who abused me had shot his girlfriend and kidnapped their baby. The victim passed away instantly from the gunshot. The perpetrator was wanted for murder and kidnapping and had been seen at a hospital pacing with the baby.

I felt so bad for the girl, her family, and most importantly, for that baby. Her family told the news reporters how he had been abusive to her and how she had tried to get away several times. The news began to read reports of other women who had come forth as his victims. They read my case without mentioning my name. All I could do was pray for the situation and give God praise for being my keeper. It is my experience that "the system" doesn't take domestic violence seriously until it is too late. Why does someone have to die at the hands of an abuser before his or her voice can be heard? When I went to the police, I was issued a PFA Protection From Abuse) paper, but what does that paper do, absolutely nothing. It shows that there is a report of abuse on file and that's about it. Nothing is ever done which is why abusers feel like they can get away with these types of situations. You have the PFA and then you call the police. By the time the police arrive, it can be too late.

An Admonition

Be careful who and what you attract into your life. A snake is not compatible with an eagle. A snake will only attract a snake. A bear will only attract a bear. A lion will only choose a lioness to help take care of and run his pack. Be confident in who you are and who God has created you to be. Being abused physically, mentally, verbally, emotionally, and even spiritually is wrong. Remove yourself from those situations immediately. Your life and others around you are depending on you.

Actress and comedienne Mo'Nique is someone who tremendously inspires me. She has a comedy special and documentary entitled "I could have been your Cellmate." She journeyed into the lives of women who were in prison for various reasons. One woman was there with her mom. The foundation of each of their stories was the same: hurt, rejection, pain, abandonment, helplessness, hopelessness or some form of abuse. I sat and watched that documentary and I cried with those women and for them.

Let me encourage you, my reader. If you are being abused in any type of way, make the best decision of your life today; leave. Get out as quickly and as safely as possible. Believe it or not ladies, we are all sisters. The world defines us by so many inadequate things. We are defined by our race, our hair, our weight, our financial status, and so much more. No matter what the world says, or how the world defines us, things like abuse, rejection, pain, and hurt have no color. They have no shape, no form. As a matter of fact, they are issues just looking for names to label them. It doesn't matter your status Abuse is abuse. Rejection is rejection. Pain is pain and hurt is hurt.

As women, we have a lot in common. When I see you I see many things about myself. I loved what Mo'Nique did with, and for those women. They probably would have never been able to tell their stories had it not been for Monique. And whether they believe it or not, their testimonies have changed the lives of others; I salute them. . Even though their situations showed that they had been incarcerated at the time, no matter where they are today, I know there will always be hope for all of them.

Contrary to popular belief, men can be, and are abused just as much as women. Domestic Violence to me is one of the biggest types of abuse that is misread and misunderstood by everyone including those involved. The perpetrator and the victim mistake it for love and attention. Outsiders looking in may mistake it for stupidity and nonsense because they have not experienced it. Trust me, I know that it is easier to tell you to get out than it is to actually leave. People risk their lives trying. Those of us that have survived and made it are now advocates for those still in the abusive places. The one and only thing that needs to shift in order to make it out, is your mindset. You must know and fully believe that you can get out and stay out. You can and will make it. If I can survive, trust me, you can too. Here are a few questions to ask yourself about your relationship.

Do you:

- feel afraid of your partner much of the time?
- avoid certain topics out of fear of angering your partner?
- feel that you can't do anything right for your partner?
- believe that you deserve to be hurt or mistreated?
- wonder if you're the one who is crazy?
- feel emotionally numb or helpless?

Does your partner do any of the following:

- have a bad and unpredictable temper?
- hurt you, or threaten to hurt or kill you?
- threaten to take your children away or harm them?
- threaten to commit suicide if you leave?
- force you to have sex?
- destroy your belongings?
- act excessively jealous and possessive?
- control where you go or what you do?
- keep you from seeing your friends or family?
- limit your access to money, the phone, or the car?
- constantly check up on you?

If you or someone you know is in an unhealthy relationship look for resources to help you safely get out. Speak with someone you trust such as your primary care physician, gynecologist, Pastor, or a counselor.

For more information you can call the National Domestic Violence Hotline: 1-800-799-(SAFE) 7233 or 911.

The National Sexual Assault Hotline: 1-800-656-4673

POLISHING THE DIAMOND

There was a time when I experienced homelessness. I was offered an opportunity to participate in a program to help me get back on my feet. In the program participants were assisted with employment and housing. Because I worked hard to complete the program and was positive the program officials allowed me to move upstairs in the shelter where I shared a room with one person instead of fourteen.

It took some time but eventually I found an affordable one-bedroom apartment in the suburbs of the city. To my surprise, my rent was only $5 a month because it was based on your income. I was unemployed at the time but I was attending school and I was in leadership training at my church. I never stayed long without a job - school, work and church helped me keep my sanity.

One particular day, I was studying the Bible in my bedroom when God spoke to me and said, "A Diamond in the Rough." Now I am a very inquisitive person by nature. If you tell me something, I have to do research, get definitions, find out the language of its origin, and dig up everything I can find. When I heard that title I immediately got excited and thought to myself, *Wow, what an awesome sermon title this is going to be!*

I began to study the definition of a diamond. It never

occurred to me that there would be a definition for A Diamond in the Rough but I was wrong. The definition for this term is:

"A precious gem or stone lacking polish or refinement."

I didn't fully understand it, but I knew it was profound. The definition spoke to me and I was excited in my research. God spoke to me and said, "No, it's bigger than that."

I was taken aback and thought to myself, *Really God, bigger than a sermon?* I thought maybe it would be the title of my first book. At a young age, I always knew that I would write a book. At one point in time, I thought it would be called, "My Testimony; the other side to the story because people always thought they had me figured out and wanted to tell my story. I said to myself, *Wow, the title of my book, now that is going to be awesome!*"

God then said again, "No, it's bigger than that."

I was really stumped. How could it be bigger than a book? God then showed me a vision of a HUGE stage with a royal blue curtain. Behind the curtain stood Bishop T.D. Jakes and a good friend named Dana. The vision did not make sense to me. I thought maybe God showed me T.D. Jakes because he hosted women's conferences. *Oh, maybe that's it. This is about s a women's conference that I am supposed to be planning.*

God said, "No, it's bigger than that. A Diamond in the Rough is you." My life has resembled a diamond that has been in the rough. Not only is this phrase the force behind the company that God wanted to birth through me, but also it is the testimony and story behind the woman that He has called me to be. I am a diamond - a rare and precious gem but I lack polish and refinement. This is a reminder of the process that I will always need God to daily pour into me and polish me. I will always need refinement from God; He will move the unwanted impurities and thoughts. The Bible says in Hebrews 9:22 "without the shedding of blood there is no remission of sins." Because of what Jesus did on the cross, we can boldly go to God for ourselves. No matter what the scars of life may look like, no matter how much we have been beaten, rejected, and torn down, God only sees the blood of his son Jesus Christ, which causes us to shine before him in His presence.

In Psalms 139:14-17 we can see that God says:

> *"For you formed my inward parts; you covered me in my mother's womb. I will praise you for I am fearfully and wonderfully made; marvelous are your works and that my soul knows very well. My frame was not hidden from you, when I was made in secret and skillfully wrought in the lowest parts of the earth. Your eyes saw my substance, being yet unformed. And in your book they all are written, the days fashioned for me, when as yet there were none of them. How precious are your thoughts to me Oh God! How great is the sum of them!"*

This scripture lets me know that His thoughts toward me are greater than anything that I can imagine. That's why He kept saying, it's bigger than that." This scripture lets me know that everything God created me to be and everything I need to survive was placed in me at the moment I was formed. How could I not love the hell out of myself? I am so in love with the passionate, adventurous and kind hearted me. So much more is being revealed.

He does this for all of us. Read in the Bible where it says, "your gifts make room for you." Don't waste time on anything that was not meant for you. Allow the unique gifts that God has placed inside of you to make room for you. Nothing and no one can change the pattern of your life unless you allow them to do so.

"Latter rain shall be greater than the former rain (Joel 2:23)." I stand on that scripture. My best days are ahead of me. I encourage you to let go of your past. Let go of the hurt. Start loving and embracing you. Is it easy? By no means, but you've got to start somewhere. One of my favorite songs by Fantasia is called, "Even Angels." Listen to it and let the chorus get in your heart. Write the vision that is on your heart; go back to school or whatever you are called to finish for God. Don't start and then quit, I encourage you to not only finish, but also FINISH STRONG! Remember God is the father of time. He is the true author and finisher of our faith. He was there in the beginning and he certainly will be there in the end. He never ends a story without bringing back the glory. Zig Ziglar reminds us in a famous quote that we just have to start and we will be great.

Taking that first leap of faith is the hardest part. There will be many questions and you will never know the endless possibilities unless you try. Stop living in the "what if" category. Take the leap of faith. Embrace each moment of everyday because you only live once. If you fall short, get back up. Remember failure is the best part of success. If you fall seven times get up 8 times.

Stop letting fear keep you in the boat. Stop letting the magnitude of fear cause you to drown. Being defeated in life is optional.

THE ANOINTING HAS A PRICE

I recently heard a friend say, "The person you are becoming is going to cost you some family, some friends, and even some places. It may cause you to lose some things, but choose her over everything." As I write this chapter, I am a living witness to these exact words. My anointing has cost me some people, places, and things that I never in a million years thought I would lose. Even as I wrote this book, I was struggling to make financial ends meet.

I decided to choose me, and I encourage you to do the same. Just like making the decision to choose that destined place, that person you are really called to be, so it is with the anointing. So much so that your flesh, your mind wanders and you question if God is there. Choose Him and the anointing over everything.

Your destiny is wrapped up in your anointing. Your purpose is wrapped up in your anointing. You can't have one without the other and in order to reach your full potential, your destined place, your purpose, you are going to have to put in some hard work. You will have to press in to God in order for your oil to flow. Once the oil flows, you will experience such a divine healing; and a victory that takes place.

What is it that God is birthing inside of you? What are you anointed to do? What is your calling in life, your destiny? Do you know what you were placed specifically on earth to do? Here are a few key things to know about yourself when it comes to your anointing:

- You were birthed with your God-given anointing already inside of you.
- When God created you, He gave you everything that you would ever need to sustain you and be successful in doing what HE has called you to do.
- Activate it, and in order to do so you must step out on faith.
- You can't fulfill your purpose without faith. The Bible instructs us to walk by faith and not by sight. Faith and reality don't mix.
- Faith is what we don't see. Reality is ever before us; it is what we do see.

Your dreams, goals and visions are BIGGER than you. They cannot be compared to reality. God did it that way so that you can depend solely on Him. Reality may reveal mountains in your way but faith says they can be removed. As I mentioned earlier, when God audibly spoke the words A Diamond in the Rough everything that I thought it was or would be was rebuffed by God when he spoke to me, "It's bigger than that."

Entrepreneurship has been a faith walk for me. Everything starts out of my own pocket. I have to remind myself everyday as I drive up and down the road and see signs for major corporations that they were all at one time a vision in someone's mind.

The bible says, NOW FAITH IS the substance of things hoped for, the evidence of things not seen. Having faith gives us substance as well as evidence. You will manifest your dreams by exercising your faith. Reality will make you believe that you are not good enough. It tells us to look at our surroundings, how can you possibly birth out a dream as big as yours with your current circumstances? For example, Moses looked at his physical ailment, the speech impairment. The first thing Moses said to God was, "Lord, I can't speak." That was his reality but God encouraged Moses to operate in faith and said, " You will speak to deliver a nation. Not just any nation, God's chosen people with four simple words, "Let my people go."

Do not allow your reality to hinder you from stepping out on faith. Allow God's purpose to be birthed inside of you. Yes, the anointing comes with a heavy cost – your old life. Your tears, pains and disappointments are worth more than what you think they are. When I think of diamonds, I always think of how expensive they are to purchase. But look at what a diamond has to go through to even get the shine that it has. Your anointing is far too expensive to let others make you hide your brightness. If you remember I told you how it wasn't money, beauty or anything wonderful that got me here. It was my pain. My tears, my heart break that allowed me to be able to write my story and manifest my dreams. I always say, "You can't tell someone that ice cream is sweet unless you have tasted it. And so it is with the diamond that you see before you today. I experienced years of sacrifice, rejection, crying when no one else was looking and many years of being overlooked, mistreated, abandoned, and abused almost to the point of death. I now know and understand, that my life is worth fighting for.

I will wear my crown well. My testimony, my scars are my badge of honor. I count my journey a privilege to have traveled thus far. And although my journey is far from complete, I am embracing my new season with an open mind, heart, and hands. Your life; my life is worth fighting for.

God spoke to me one morning in prayer about how we approach Him. He said this to me:

> "When you come to Me, you must come with an open mind, open heart, and open hands ready to receive from me. I will pour back into you everything that you need so

> you can give. I long to bless my children but you must be in a posture to receive. Sometimes you come into My presence bogged down with your unnecessary weights. Be careful to leave those weights at my feet where they belong. I can't bless you when your hands, hearts and minds are full. Release and receive."

If your cup is always full, there is no way God can restore you. Every encounter with God should be a change or exchange. You don't want to come in contact with God and expect to be the same. No flesh, no weight, no sickness, no disease, NOTHING of this world can survive in his presence. His spirit alone is enough to cure a nation, to break chains in both the earthly and the spiritual realms. God Alone IS ENOUGH.

I encourage you to put it all in His hands. I have made a list and daily I add to it things I need to give back to him. Do this activity:

- Make your list of things you want to give back to God. Pray for an understanding of your purpose.
- Ask God what your next move will be. Most importantly ask Him how you can find and be your own peace. Loving YOU is free. This, my friend is the key ingredient to a successful story that you will live and write.

EMBRACING ME

New.

In the Biblical passage of II Corinthians 5:17 is a great explanation of what it new means: “Old things have passed away and behold all things become new.” Starting something fresh is not as easy as it sounds. Although it may seem exciting and wonderful at first thought, there is a lot that comes with it.

When you start something new that means whatever happened or took place prior to this "new thing" is gone or at least no longer should be in your thoughts. If the old stuff is still a part of your life, you will never be able to move forward in the new. Once you’re in the new, it is a learning experience. You have to undergo a learning experience when you arrive at the new phase. It can be a new job; a new house; a new appliance; a new marriage or a new mindset you have to efficiently adjust to learn how to think and operate in your newness.

I was thirty-nine when I experienced a new ness for myself. My life up until that point had been in existence for everyone else. Because of the way that I grew up, no one told me how important it was to love myself in order to be an effective person. The gift of my kind heart and good nature that everyone loved became one of my biggest areas of growth.

Being a kind-hearted person has its ups and downs. One of the greatest misconceptions that I often face is people who think I am weak. That is a lie. In fact, I am a living witness that we may be some of the strongest people in the world. While we are being kind to others, while we are smiling, encouraging and wiping other people's tears, we want to cry too! We want to scream and fall apart but we don't.

I am kind hearted, however for most of my life I have dealt with the effects of the rejection I experienced as a child. Rejection has caused me to second guess myself, question my gifts/talents and keep my heart's desires hidden. It caused me to look for love in the wrong places, love the wrong people, and allow the wrong people to love me. Because I experienced rejection for so long I was fearful of becoming something great. Every rejection created a void in my life, which caused me to reject myself.

I didn't know how to love myself. All of the love that I had, I poured onto others instead of pouring it into me. My best friend would always say to me, "Qi, everyone is not like you, so you can't expect people to return on the same level as you." I would outwardly agree with her but internally I was hurt and rejected by her insight. I didn't understand at the time why it would not be reciprocal.

You may be wondering how I rejected myself. I am glad you asked. My closest friends will tell you that I have done nothing but make sacrifices just to give to others. I would never take time for myself. I had been rejected since childhood and I didn't know how to love or embrace myself. I was actually afraid to. I was actually giving away what I needed to develop and embrace inside of me by pouring it out into others.

I helped everyone else birth their dreams and live out their happiness. I lived by the old mantra that tells us we should "treat people how you want to be treated." My belief was that if I stood on that principle I would be blessed in return. While that statement is true and I still live by it today, when I initially learned of it I thought that people were going to give me back 100 percent of what I gave them in time, money, attention, or love. I came to understand that my best friend had been right all along. Boy, did I get a rude awakening. Not only did it not come back to me, People actually treated me worse. There were years of sleepless nights, crying, hurt, pain, and a lot of money that I can't get back even if I tried. The problem with that lifestyle is while I was taking care of everybody else; no one was taking care of me - not even me. I was wiping other people's tears away while internally crying my own. Never once did I think about myself the way that I really should have. I showed people how to love me with the way I loved myself and I was not very good at it.

I wanted someone to hear my silent cries but how can anyone hear a cry if it is silent?

When I began to understand what it means to embrace, I had to study the word. The word "embrace" has several definitions. The first definition is "To hold someone closely in one's arms; especially as a sign of affection." As I looked at the first definition of the word embrace and worked on this chapter in my book, my mind went back to a talk show that Emmy award-winning actress Mo'Nique hosted on BET with comedienne Rodney Perry. She would always tell her studio audience and the viewers watching at the end of the show to wrap their arms around themselves and hug themselves. She would say, "I love you for free Suga." That pierced me in my heart and when I experienced my new day everything became new about me.

The first time that I saw Mo'Nique perform she was hilariously funny to me. I was drawn to her message about self-love and affirmation as a plus-sized woman. It was eye opening for me to finally get to see someone who looked like me in real life, doing her thing on a national platform without shame. It made me feel great. I began to follow her career and I realized her message was more than just about being a confident big girl and being cute, but it was about all women embracing our God-given beauty no matter what size, color, or shape we are. From Mo'Nique I understood how to embrace and love the woman God created me to be.

The second definition of the word "embrace" is actually my favorite of the ones I researched:

> "To accept or support a belief, theory, or change willingly or enthusiastically."

After all those years of feeling unloved, unwanted, defeated, I decided to willingly accept or embrace who I am with enthusiasm. I have made a conscious decision to simply, live. I've been hearing different phrases lately such as "You only live once." What I find ironic is that I now know I was always in a PROCESS to embrace the woman God created me to be, but I was blind to it. A person once told me that I was jealous of the relationship she had with her son because I hadn't been loved the way that they loved one another. Those words hurt me but it was not my truth. Although I went through some crazy things, one thing that I never lacked was love. I did not get to see my mother often in the adolescent phase of my life and the times that I did see her were strained yet I never lacked motherly love or the strength of a woman's presence.

These women were there for me during different times throughout my life. They made sure that I was in church, that I was praying and covered in prayer, and to help me understand simple things like how to wash up and brush my teeth. These women made sure I knew how to clean my face properly by teaching me facials. An angel taught me how to cook a meal, and how to dress. Family members and peers had torn me down and called me ugly for so long that I started to believe them. I will forever be grateful for the older women who would always tell me how pretty I am. I had a hard time accepting their compliments because of the negativity around me but they were consistent to build me up.

My angels, these women are true DIAMONDS for building me up, confronting the negative attacks against me and for taking the time to check on me. It's because of women like them that I am able to shine today and embrace all of me in authentic love. I shine because they have allowed me to shine. To this day, God is adding to my collection of GEMS but my angels are my foundation.

I find myself learning how to increase my self-love. I am accepting how all of my failures, mistakes, and heartaches have shaped me. I am learning what I like and what I love. I am now embracing all of my entire process with a smile. I embrace it knowing that because of my journey, I am now evolving into the woman that God has purposed me to be. I am now someone who takes care of herself first. I am starting to live for ME.

There has been many times throughout my life that I thought that statement was selfish. How can you simply live for you? How can I live for me when people, especially my children need and depend on me? I remember when my sons were born. I knew and felt at the time that I had to live for them. My life no longer mattered. Everything about me had to do with them. But now I think to myself, how foolish was that thinking? If I don't take care of myself, live, and be happy how can I ever possibly live for and take care of my boys? Taking care of me is a part of taking care of them. The best love that we can show anyone is our self-love.

From my experience I hope that you will stop planting seeds of low self-esteem, doubt, fear and lack of love into yourselves and your children. We set the standard for how people treat us and how they treat our children. I am raising my boys to be good citizens in society, great fathers, but most importantly phenomenal husbands and true men of God. How can they be all of that without properly knowing, embracing, and loving themselves for who God created them to be? Let me tell you, I don't care how beautiful you may think you are, I don't care if you drive the best cars, live in the fanciest house, or wear the most expensive clothing, without self-love you are lacking. There will always be a void that will need to be filled. A void that money can't buy and clothes can't cover up. No matter what lie you tell yourself, people are going to notice that void and will prey on your weakness.

God is calling you to LIVE, LOVE, and LET GO. Live like there is no tomorrow, Love until you can't love anymore, and let go of all of the people, places, and things that have hindered you or are trying to stop you from being the BEST YOU that you can be. There was a group called TLC who sings a song called "Unpretty." I encourage you to listen to the chorus, which is a declaration that the only one who can make you feel less than adequate is yourself.

I have made plenty mistakes, I am not perfect. No one is perfect but God. Remember that the definition of a "diamond in the rough" teaches us that we lack polish and refinement. Even embracing those times that you mess up and fall short is a part of the process in loving and becoming a better you.

The process was long and challenging but I can say that I now embrace all of me. I absolutely love every flaw, every bump, and every curve about me. I am confident in the woman that God has made me. Where there was once fear, there is now peace. Now I can tell people if they have a problem with me, they have to take it up with my heavenly father. After all, He is the one who designed and created me, and I AM a diamond. To be honest, I don't think I could have ever grasped the part of being unbreakable until I had been broken.

MY JOURNEY, MY PEACE UNBREAKABLE

I remember as a little girl having a dream that I was being stabbed and cut with a knife by a group of people while standing outside of a big white house. There were wounds all over my body from head to toe and I was crying because I did not understand why I was being cut, or why I was being abused to that degree. After a while I cried out to the crowd, "There is nowhere else for you to cut me." When I woke up from my dream I recall how real the experience had felt to me. My body was a little sore, but I had no marks on me.

Now I understand that through the years those wounds in my dream were wounds that had been caused by all of the agony endured throughout my life. There were several times that I felt as if I was hanging on to my sanity by a piece thread or that I would die. On one occasion, I attempted to take my life because of all of the pain. I was tired of being homeless. I was tired of always being the one to give, encourage, and build others up without it being reciprocated to me. No one could see that I was hurting. At least they didn't tell me if they did.

When Pastor Jackie preached the sermon, "Bend, and don't break" it was developing a seed of faith in me. Now when I get asked how I made it I think to myself, *I haven't made it.* Statistics or the secular world would say that because of my upbringing I should have always been in poverty or the welfare system, I should be mentally unstable, strung out on drugs, have a bunch of children with multiple fathers, or dead. I am alive and well and I am still defeating the odds that were set against me.

Now that I am experiencing peace I can tell you that it is important to be honest with yourself when you are in pain, need a hug, or need assistance. There will be times when you need to emphatically say, "No."

This is how you love and take care of yourself first. Taking care of yourself means giving back to you what is needed to sustain and keep you mentally, emotionally, spiritually, and physically happy. It means living your life to the fullest with no regrets. Taking care of yourself means that you are reaching toward your highest height and accepting you for who God created you to be - flaws and all. It means doing what you think is impossible because with God all things are possible.

As I stated before, a diamond is not a diamond without going through a process. Unlike many other gems, it is well-suited to daily wear because of its resistance to scratching—perhaps contributing to its popularity as the preferred gem in engagement or wedding rings, which are often worn every day. When polished, diamonds maintain their shine.

God told me to tell you, IT WAS NECESSARY! Every bump, bruise, scar, high place, and low place was necessary. Be proud of your battle scars. I know, it was pain that got us here, but our pain produced our purpose. Thank God for the wounds that are now healed yet beautifully scarred. Wear them well and tell the story of how you made it through because of God.

Everything I have experienced has allowed me to be the beautiful and precious gem that people know and love today. I thank God for using my mistakes to make me who I am. As you think about your own journey, I want to break down a few key words for you. I told you I am a researcher. Hopefully these words will help you understand your journey to peace and your durability as a diamond.

Hardness

According to Wikipedia, A diamond is the hardest known natural material on both the Vickers and Mohs scale. A diamond's hardness has been known since antiquity, and is the source of its name. The hardness of diamond contributes to its suitability as a gemstone. Only diamonds can scratch other diamonds.

Unbreakable

One of the best features about a diamond is the fact that it is not easily broken. A diamond rarely breaks. The only thing that will break a diamond is an engineering tool such as a hammer. In order for a hammer to be used, someone has to literally hold it and hit it against the object. The term broken is the past particle of break. Let's look into this further:

- When there is a break it's already broken
- A break means having been (past tense again) fractured or damaged and no longer in one-piece or in working order.

Unlike a diamond, people have feelings. How many times have we allowed the enemy to infiltrate our lives? How many times have we allowed him to come in and break us? Yes, we were born into sin, but again, thank you Jesus for His blood that has redeemed us and set us free. When we are broken we may give up hope or feel despair (beaten, defeated, subdued). Maybe something happened when you were young. As I write this, I hear rape, molestation, victims of abuse, beaten, low self-esteem, maybe you were forced to grow up early, people lied to you, talked about you, ridiculed you, whatever it was that broke you, Fill in the blank_____________.

The only way we as human forms of God's diamonds can break is if we let someone else break us. We can only be broken if we allow the things that other people say and do define us.

The scripture says, when I am afraid, I will trust in you. I have learned to trust in God. It sounds like a cliché' I know, but when that is all I had, that as all I could do. When God created us, we were made whole, complete in His image. It is not easy to walk around as a broken person. It not only further damages you if you're not healed, but it also seeks to destroy everything and everyone in your path. Even though it may have been a person or people that may have caused the damage, the Bible says that we do not wrestle against flesh and blood.

The Bible says in John 10:10 the enemy comes to rob us of things that were meant to prosper us.

> *"The thief comes to steal, kill and destroy but I come that they may have life and have it more abundantly."*

What is meant to prosper us? I am glad that you asked. Most people think that if you have money, you are set. You have arrived and are prosperous. Grant it, money is wonderful to have, but it will only get you so far. There is not an amount of money that can buy hope, peace, love, or joy.

So what does the enemy do? The enemy comes in to steal those things that we easily give up. We will hold on to our expensive things, but will give up so easily on mandatory things like peace. With that, the enemy steals our confidence. He comes into the home and disrupts it. Demonic spirits are sent to attack our physical being and cause lifetime wounds.

Wounds

As I write this part of the chapter I am reminded of a conference that I hosted with a theme of "Broken, But Healed." You see, wounds hurt whether we acknowledge them or ignore them.

What is a wound? A wound is an injury to a living tissue caused by a cut, blow, or other impact typically one in which the skin is cut or broken. The first phase of the wound is the initial hurt. Whenever a person has broken skin they will experience blood rushing to the site of the impact to immediately start the healing process. At the initial impact of the wound it usually will bleed and some form of pressure is applied to the wound to stop the bleeding and ease the pain. Think about how when a woman is in labor her skin often tears while giving birth or the obstetrician has to cut her to make the hole big enough for the baby's head. Once dilated, she then pushes (applies her own pressure) against the pain to give birth to the seed.

I believe it is the same way in the spirit realm when we are hurting and wounded. The blood that was shed on the cross rushes to aid us. It is there whenever we need it. As a matter of fact, God knew that we would need it so He sent an advance on the down payment for our lives. But we again, must do our part. We have to make sure we are not just bleeding out. We have to make sure that the blood that was shed for us is not being wasted. The blood of Jesus will always fulfill its duty, but we have to be receptive of it.

All wounds need to be cleaned to encourage proper healing. Some wounds may just need to be cleaned up with peroxide and a Band-Aid, while others may need stitches. In worse case scenarios, some wounds need to be stitched back together in surgery. It all depends upon the depth of the hurt. Once the wound is properly cleaned, bandaged, and wrapped up it can properly heal.

Once the wound has been cleaned up, bleeding has ceased and pressure has been applied, there is a scar. This is evidence that you have been wounded. Some wounds are lifetime scars. Others are scars that can no longer physically be seen, but the reminder of the hurt remains. This is part of the healing process.

Once a decision is made that you want to heal, and are willing to be healed, the healing can begin. One must be very careful during the initial phase of the healing process. You see, if you bump up against the wound, you can cause pain and may even cause it to bleed again. You can interrupt the healing process and may have to go back to the doctor to have them fix the damage.

Wounds are unfortunately a part of life. In order to become who we want to be and who God created us to be, we have to incur bumps and bruises along the way. I am grateful to God for every wound, each one carries it's own weight. However, if we are not careful, the enemy can use wounds as stumbling blocks to keep us bound, angry, bitter, and hurting.

Jesus: Our Example

One person who can truly relate to having scars is Jesus Christ. Even His wounds were necessary. We were so important to Him that He was wounded for our transgressions. (Isaiah 53:5). Jesus is our healing balm. So, what am I truly saying about being unbreakable. First in order to know that you are unbreakable, you must be broken. Not just broken, but be broken down to what you feel is beyond repair. You must be in a place where you are lower than what you thought your lowest place would be. What we see is not what God sees. The Bible says that his thoughts are higher than ours and His ways are not our ways.

I have and I am sure that most of you reading this book may have said at one time or another, "I can't take it anymore." You were at the point of hanging on by a thread. I know that feeling. Many times I have imagined myself hanging and holding onto a thin piece of thread. I would cry and encourage myself, "With God

I can make it."

God knows how much you can take. Just like a boxer in the ring who keeps getting hit by his opponent, he may be thinking, "I'm still on my feet, but I can't take anymore hits." The referee steps in just in the nick of time, but when he steps in, he wraps his arm around the fighter who is hurting and protects him from the opponent by calling the fight. That is just how God does us.

You can be unbreakable until you have reached the point of being so broken that you can't take any more hits. Once God repairs you, you come into the understanding that you are unbreakable. If you were breakable you would have given up. Thank God for the Holy Spirit, the part that makes the puzzle whole to make sure you are not broken beyond repair.

Declaring to be Unbreakable

Don't you dare give up! You must endure, live and hold on while you feel yourself breaking. On the other side of your break is through. Hold your head up high and believe that there is a blessing on the other side but you have to go through the process. In one of his songs Michael Jackson sings, "It is so high you can't get over it. It is so low you can't get under it." This is what having a process feels like. You must go through the process and endure until it is completed. While the enemy tries everything that he can to break you, remember God's promises and that He is setting you up for the breakthrough you are praying for.

Read these declarations aloud:

- The Holy Spirit is in His rightful place lifting up a standard for me. I AM UNBREAKABLE.
- God is with me and I will make it to the breakthrough. I AM UNBREAKABLE.
- I may feel the hurt at times but I AM UNBREAKABLE.
- I will keep pressing when I feel like I am at the end of my rope. I AM UNBREAKABLE.
- I LOVE MYSELF ENOUGH to stand on the truth that I AM UNBREAKABLE.
- If no one else stays or stands with me, I AM UNBREAKABLE.

EPILOGUE: EMBRACING THE PROCESS

"NOW faith is the substance of things hoped for and the evidence of things not seen."

(Hebrews 11:1)

This scripture says so much in so few words about the process. It starts with the word now, which means "at the present time or moment." Your "Now Faith" is going to determine the very moment that you are experiencing in your process of growth. Faith is the foundation of the process.

Although I experienced physical abuse, hurt, and rejection at a young age, I never wavered in my faith. I always knew that it would get better for us. I never saw myself in the moment where bad things were happening to me. Where I am spiritually, physically and emotionally is a result of how I saw myself years ago. I saw my book even when I had no words for it yet.

I know where I want to go on this journey called life, but I also know that this journey is going to take a process in order to get there. I may not know the blueprint of the process, or what the process may hold, but I know that every single part of the process is needed to not only get me to where God wants me to be, but to help me to sustain and maintain while I'm in my victory season.

There is so much more to my story. Can you believe it, even more than this? But guess what, even in victory, there is still a process.

So, how do we embrace the process?

Remember, embrace means to accept or support change willingly or enthusiastically. We will always have big dreams, big hopes. We may want to be entrepreneurs with fortune 500 companies, or doctors, lawyers, or we may want to start a foundation and give back to the community. It's a beautiful thought isn't it? I mean we really see this thing and the potential of where it's going to go and who will be blessed by it. But we never take into consideration the long hours, the countless days, weeks, months, or years. There is paperwork to file to become a legal organization not to mention the state, city, and federal government taxes to file.

What about school? We see the Doctorate or Master's degree and forget about the hours of study, the papers and tests. Let's not even talk about the money for school. That begins another series of questions for me.

No one told me as an entrepreneur that I was going to have to take from myself. No one told me that a lot of times I would have to walk alone. I was not advised that others would not see my vision or treat my vision the way that I do. I did not fathom that there would be days that I would struggle financially and have to miss important things like empowerment conferences or financial seminars because the funds just would not be there.

It was not on my mind to think about how my nine to five job in corporate America would fund my home life and my business. Life coach, and author Iyanla Vanzant she says one phrase in the opening credits of her show "Fix my Life" that now and will forever tug on the core of my heart. She says, "You've got to do the work." I have put in the time, effort, and the sacrifices for my peace. I did my work and I want to help you do your work.

Embracing the process is not easy. Don't give up with the thought of having to go through so much to obtain victory. I promise you, if you embrace the process enthusiastically by doing the work and making your faith your foundation, the sky will never be the limit for you. There are NO LIMITS on what one can achieve with God. Don't ever limit yourself. Speak what you want so that you will have what you say. This my friend is "Now Faith." You need it to help you on your journey and to have your peace along the way.

PART III: TOOLS FOR THE PROCESS

SCRIPTURES

- Hebrews 9:22
- Hebrews 11:1
- Psalm 139: 14-17
- Romans 8:28
- Joel 2:23
- II Corinthians 5:17
- Isaiah 53:5
- Isaiah 55:8-9
- 1 Kings 17
- Jeremiah 23:11
- Ephesians 6
- John 10:10
- Psalm 56:3
- Deuteronomy 7:6-9

REFLECTION SONGS

- The Winans, "Millions"
- The Winans, "Ain't no Need to Worry"
- The Winans, "It's Gonna Be Alright"
- Tupac, "Keep Ya Head Up"
- Yolanda Adams, "Still I Rise"
- Fantasia, "It was Necessary"
- TLC, "Unpretty"
- Tasha Cobb, "I have decided"
- Yolanda Adams, "I Gotta Believe"
- Donnie McClurkin, "We Fall Down"
- James Fortune, "I Will Trust"
- Fantasia, "Even Angels"
- Kirk Franklin, "Imagine Me"

ABOUT THE AUTHOR

"Life is not about waiting for the storm to pass,
but learning to dance in the rain."
~Vivian Green

Survivor. Believer. Strong. Loving. Qiana Buckner is a living testimony of God's mercy and grace. Having endured many hardships as a child from growing up in the foster care system, experiencing homelessness, suffering from physical, verbal and mental abuse, she believes whole heartedly in the power of God's redemption. Qiana learned to lean on God's promises and that has kept her strong throughout her life.

Qiana is inspired by her wonderful children, Kevin and Korey. She calls them her heartbeats and loves to be their biggest cheerleader when they play sports.

As an entrepreneur Qiana implements passion projects such as Diamonds and Debutants (a mentoring program), Gifts for Grads, and expositions for Education, Health and Wellness. She is the CEO and Founder of A Diamond in the Rough Productions, which is an event planning company. Her accomplishments through A Diamond in the Rough have impacted individuals, communities and organizations.

Ms. Buckner prides herself on collaborating with others to help them achieve their God-given purpose. She spread's God's love through her involvement with several community, church and civic organizations and is a proud dignitary of Theta Phi Sigma Christian Sorority, Incorporated. In addition to all of these service endeavors, Qiana serves as Vice President of the Board of Directors for Penn Hills Charter School of Entrepreneurship.

When talking about her legacy Qiana is humble, "I want people to remember me as a woman of integrity and character who loved others to the fullest extent possible." She is thoughtful about her experiences, "I have always been determined to win at life no matter what."

Made in the USA
Middletown, DE
24 August 2020

16757778R00086